The Boatman: An Indian Love Story

Touching, honest, and brave, *The Boatman* draws us irresistibly into an intense new world. Vivid descriptions and a heady pace never let the reader go.

Dianne Highbridge, *A Much Younger Man*
and *In the Empire of Dreams*

Burbidge's book is immensely educative and should be compulsory reading on how a foreigner discovers his true nature but returns home a very strong and confident man in charge of his life. *The Boatman* will surely take you across the Ganga.

Ashok Row Kavi, *Hindustan Times*

An engrossing, often disturbing, story, grippingly told. It is both every gay man's story and unlike any you've ever read.

Robert Dessaix, writer and critic

This tender story of naked lust and obsessive craving is as intoxicating as India itself. It made me want to return there.

Benjamin Law, *Gaysia* and *The Family Law*

Unexpectedly contemporaneous, while still managing to evoke the ethos of a country in flux — the early profusion of exotica giving way to a more observed understanding of India.

Vikram Phukan, *TimeOut Mumbai*

A charming account of an unspoken side of life in Mumbai in the eighties. Its strength lies in its unique perspective. Instead of coming out to his mother, he seems to come out to India.

Mahesh Dattani, playwright, director & actor

While most urban gay men in 80s India might have fantasized about going to explore their sexuality in the West, Burbidge stumbles upon the reverse journey, which he tells with great honesty. It would have been easier to write an exciting book about a foreigner's adventures in India. This is far more nuanced and is all the more touching for it.

Sandip Roy, *Firstpost.com*

For a country that still criminalizes homosexuality, *The Boatman* chronicles its own cities that defy the law every night as spaces morph, people emerge and all types of liaisons are made and broken.

Priyanka Kotamraju, *The Hindu*

Burbidge took shocking risks in exploring his homosexuality and found a capacity for the covert that both fascinated and appalled him. Along with his compassionate and respectful depiction of Indian street life and a hunger for discovery, this makes for a memorable read.

Jen Banyard, *Spider Lies* and the *Riddle Gully* series

Dare Me! The Life and Work of Gerald Glaskin

John Burbidge's biography is one of the best yet written about an Australian writer.

David Hough, *The West Australian*

Burbidge has done us a favor in bringing an important writer back to the spotlight, and recounting a life that reveals much about marginality in twentieth century Australia.

Dennis Altman, *Homosexual: Oppression and Liberation*

A grand story masterfully told. His management of detail is one of its strengths — quite an amazing accomplishment.

Robert Dessaix, writer and critic

This impressive research brings Glaskin back from near oblivion. Burbidge gives us Glaskin with all his charm as well as his furious obstinacy.

Jeremy Fisher, *The Australian Book Review*

John Burbidge's biography rescues Glaskin from obscurity and uses his life to throw light on a period of Australian history that is attracting more and more attention.

Graham Willett, *Australian Lesbian and Gay Archives*

Vividly presented in the many circumstances of a warring but productive life, Glaskin has well merited Burbidge's entertaining and scrupulous attention.

Peter Pierce, *The Weekend Australian*

Burbidge's detailed biography is an intriguing read for anyone who wants to gain a good sense of what Western Australian life was like in decades gone by, and an insightful view into queer life in Perth prior to the decriminalization of homosexuality.

Graeme Watson, *OutinPerth*

The sensitivity, respect and understanding Burbidge has brought to Glaskin's life and work is enormous. No doubt Glaskin would have berated or corrected Burbidge, but he could not help but have been proud and grateful to be so well understood and so generously described.

Jo Darbyshire, Curator, *The Gay Museum*, Western Australia

MORE THAN HALFWAY TO SOMEWHERE

Collected Gems of a World Traveler

Back Story to the Front Cover

In 2013 my husband and I were hiking in the Mojanda Lakes in Ecuador. We'd been walking all day, hadn't seen a soul, and with only a handwritten map we weren't sure exactly where we were. The afternoon was fast disappearing and we still had a way to go.

Then we arrived at a three-way intersection and found a sign detached from its post. It puzzled us. Were we 6.3 km into a 9.5 km section of the trail or did we still have 6.3 km to go? What would we find when we got there? And in which direction was the sign meant to be pointing?

Despite our perplexity and growing anxiety, we were able to laugh at our situation. Traveling is full of surprises and a little humor helps. When choosing a title for this book, we were reminded of this occasion and decided to honor it with *More Than Halfway to Somewhere*.

Also by John Burbidge

Approaches That Work in Rural Development

*Beyond Prince and Merchant: Citizen Participation
and the Rise of Civil Society*

Please Forward: The Life of Liza Tod

Dare Me! The Life and Work of Gerald Glaskin

The Boatman: An Indian Love Story

To Karen & Daniel —

MORE THAN HALFWAY TO SOMEWHERE

Collected Gems of a World Traveler

Enjoy the ride!

Best,
John

John Burbidge

Wordswallah Publishing
488 Reed Bay Road
Decatur Island WA 98221
USA
www.wordswallah.com

Cover design and layout by
Robert Lanphear, Lanphear Design
www.lanpheardesign.com

Cover image of author: Bruce Robertson

Background cover image: OllirgPhoto

ISBN: 978-0-578-69814-4

For Duncan

Travel does not merely broaden the mind.
It makes the mind.

Bruce Chatwin, *Anatomy of Restlessness*

. . . . .

At the end of our lives,
all we will have left behind are our stories.

Brad Newsham, *A Sense of Place*

CONTENTS

. . . . .

Acknowledgments

· · · · ·

This collection of stories has endured an unusually long gestation and undergone several abortions. It was shunted to the back burner more than once as other books took precedence. When several writing and publishing friends convinced me it wasn't a commercial proposition, I nearly gave up on it. It might never have been born at all, had it not been for the support and encouragement of a number of people.

Among those I would like to acknowledge are Sandy Conant Strachan, for agreeing to write a foreword and offering invaluable advice from her own finely honed writing skills; Suzanne Falkiner, for critiquing the manuscript and suggesting numerous ways to improve it; Karyle Kramer, Taylor West and Patt Wilson from the Whidbey Island Writers Association who helped me produce and refine early drafts of stories; and Jan Clifford, Peter Goers, Robyn Hutchinson, Nancy Lanphear and John Telford, whose affirmative responses helped me overcome my doubts about the project.

I was delighted to secure Bob Lanphear's graphic design skills, which added immensely to the quality of this publication. I'm also most grateful to those who kindly agreed to lend me their images when I lacked my own, including Sam Dorrance, Yann Forget, Johan Ljungdahl, Jerry Riley, Peter Romberg and Ann Voli.

Foreword

. . . . .

When John asked me to write a foreword, I immediately said yes. I've known John for forty years or more and have been there for a few of the events he describes in his stories. I have found him to be an unfailingly kind, gentle, curious man, but I would never have described him as 'intrepid'. These stories are evidence that I left something out!

What follows are anecdotes from an adventurous life, one lived with a willingness to fully engage — with people, circumstances, the unknown. A willingness to let life unfold and to learn from it. An amazing memory for the details, color, humor and pathos of many different experiences. I am struck with how many risky moments he's had in places like Nigeria and India. But his resilience has been proven throughout, and even more important, he's gleaned 'meaning' from his encounters with danger and uncertainty. He has appreciated the people he's met and brought them to life.

I'm confident these stories will allow every reader to laugh, to be frightened or confused, to accept diversity, to keep a perspective. Some like myself will see history play out in a friend's life. Others will be amazed at the panorama of experiences one person can have. Still others will feel a twinge of regret at what they missed. The stories provide a window onto the incredible world and the humanity we share.

So it's with great pleasure that I recommend this book. If your own life has been more sedate, you'll have an opportunity to experience fresh challenges. If your life has been an adventure, you'll accompany John on his unique expedition. Enjoy this journey across our planet with a very special man!

Sandy Conant Strachan
San Jose, Costa Rica
March 2020

Introduction

· · · · ·

Early one Friday morning in March 1977 I stood by the roadside in India and watched bus after bus pass by our village. Indian buses are always full but this day broke all records. With bodies crammed into every crevice, along with caged chickens, bulging bundles and other paraphernalia on top, this procession of buses was like a circus on the move. Finally one stopped, and with two of my Indian colleagues pushing from behind I managed to get a toehold on the bottom step of the rear doorway. When we arrived in Yeotmal an hour and a half later I was relieved to sit down but even more thankful to be alive.

I had little trouble finding a bus out of Yeotmal to my final destination. As we rattled along I noticed that villages looked unusually tidy and were adorned with political slogans and massive face paintings of Indira Gandhi. Eastern Maharashtra was one of her strongholds, where she regularly attracted crowds of 100,000 or more. Although I'd been in India a few months, my work in villages had isolated me from the political unrest sweeping the country. Indira's imposition of a state of emergency had caused great turmoil and led her to call an election to consolidate her faltering grip on power.

We hadn't gone far when our bus entered a village festooned with archways of marigolds and bunting laden with Indian flags. As the bus pulled off the road, the conductor made an announcement in Marathi, after which passengers filed out of the bus. Some made for the nearest chai stand while others kept peering down the road. I turned to the man next to me and asked what was going on.

"Madam is coming!" he replied excitedly, as if another Bollywood blockbuster was about to burst onto the screen.

Twenty minutes passed. An eerie silence descended on the village. All of a sudden quiet chatter turned into agitated speech. People jumped up and moved around. A truck disgorged a load of lathi-wielding policemen who ushered the crowd back from the roadside. As a cavalcade of vehicles came roaring toward us I jostled my way to the front to get a clearer view.

Fifth in line behind police jeeps and Ambassadors laden with Congress-I politicians was a cream-colored 1950s Cadillac with tail fins. In the front passenger seat, sari draped over her forehead, she sat like a goddess in her chariot, albeit a rather incongruous chariot given her government's espoused opposition to imported goods. But this was India, where paradoxes abound and exceptions are often the rule.

As her car passed she glanced in my direction. For the briefest moment our eyes locked. A puzzled look came over her face, as if to say, "Who on earth are you and what are you doing here?" She might also have been saying, as she often did, "Foreign hands are everywhere, meddling in our country. Check out that character in the dark blue safari suit."

I felt like I was in a fairy tale, but was she the fairy godmother or the wicked witch? Some thought one, some the other. She would go on to lose this election and later her life. But this fleeting encounter would remain with me, reminding me that I was a stranger in a strange land, trying hard to fit in when so clearly I didn't. This would become a defining motif in my life. Indeed, it always has been.

* * *

I had come to India to take part in an ambitious undertaking called the Maharashtra Village Development Project conducted by the Institute of Cultural Affairs (ICA), an NGO with which I volunteered. An offshoot of the Christian-based Ecumenical Institute, the ICA pioneered a radically new, people-centered approach to community and organizational development that became known as the 'technology of participation'. As society unraveled around us it was just the kind of thing that attracted young people like me who wanted to make a difference. A university student in Australia in the late '60s, I'd been involved in anti-Vietnam war protests, the Aboriginal land rights campaign and the activist Student Christian Movement. But these efforts were piecemeal and short-range. I was yearning for something more comprehensive and long-term. Along came the Institute calling for 'a new social vehicle' and 'a new religious mode.' I signed up.

A unique feature of the Institute was that its full-time staff lived communally. Modeled on religious orders, families and individuals in each location lived under one roof with common timetables, meals and finances, which included a minimal stipend but no salary. Some staff in each location were assigned to 'work out' to bring in income for the entire community, while others focused full time on program activities with churches and communities. During my intern year in Perth I was assigned to get a job and after weeks of trying ended up as a probation and parole officer. I can't imagine work I was less suited for. Although I was 22, I looked 16. When I'd meet clients for the first time they would assume I was some flunky whose job was to escort them to the real officer. Prison visits were a nightmare and house calls were mostly to parts of Perth I'd never set foot in. When the chance to go to Chicago came after eight months, I promptly resigned.

My reason for going to Chicago was to undertake a six-month internship with the Institute, after which I intended to return to Australia. The first two months involved a residential program called The Global Academy. This novel creation was an eclectic mix of lectures, seminars and workshops that used writings of state-of-the-art thinkers from a range of disciplines. But there were no term papers or grades. The Academy confronted participants with a broad swath of contemporary wisdom on a range of social, cultural and ethical issues, then posed the question of how we might respond to them. We spent eight weeks in a windowless building in the ghetto and were allowed out in groups on Wednesday and Sunday afternoons. If you were foolish enough to venture forth on your own your chances of being mugged, or worse, were almost guaranteed.

After the Academy I spent several months teaching in a preschool that was part of the community revitalization project the Institute had undertaken with neighborhood residents. I was assigned to work with a large black woman whose bark would peel paint off the wall. She was one of several local women who worked alongside Institute staff to give the youngest members of this eviscerated community a head start in life. The curriculum was an innovative mix of the basics with an infusion of songs, stories and rituals. It was designed to transform the image of ghetto kids as 'a lost cause' into one in which they could take charge of their lives and carve out a positive future. With racism still rife in America, this was an audacious act.

The third component of my internship was my first chance to experience America beyond the ghetto. I was given a $99 Greyhound bus ticket and sent on a tour of Institute offices across the US and Canada. I woke up the first morning in Madison, Wisconsin to hear birds chirping instead of the deafening sound of cars racing down the expressway. When I returned to Chicago several months later, the ghetto was transformed. Summer had arrived, trees were covered with leaves, and children played in water spewing from fire hydrants.

When my US visa expired for the third and last time, I wasn't ready to return to Australia. I was asked to go to Toronto where, again assigned to 'work out', I became the administrator of a government-funded project that provided home-help services to the aged and infirmed. Just before the grant finished and the project closed I became a Canadian Landed Immigrant, but wasn't able to take advantage of this new status. In the early hours of a damp July morning in 1974 I received a phone call that my father had died, aged 58. I resigned from two part-time jobs and boarded the first of five planes for the 35-hour journey to Perth. My mother was shattered by my father's death, so I stayed with her for a couple of months to help her recover and adjust to her new life.

* * *

By this time the Institute had begun working with Aboriginal communities in northwestern Australia, one of which was a former mission that had closed in the 1960s, leading most of the population to relocate to the nearby town where they succumbed to alcohol abuse, violence and prostitution. When some of the elders decided they'd had enough, a sympathetic community welfare officer supported their efforts to return to their tribal land and invited the Institute to help them rebuild their community. The federal government offered grants for such 'back to the land' movements and they were a lucky recipient.

I was asked to come to fill in for one of two teachers who was leaving, until a 'proper' teacher was found. The day I arrived the departing teacher briefed me on my role before she left the following morning. I struggled to create lesson plans and get to know my students, which was difficult because the same ones didn't show up every day. My saving grace in this baptism of fire was my 'teaching assistant', an obese young Aboriginal man with thighs like a horse and whose commands got the immediate attention of any child. He had strong self-esteem and a no-bullshit manner, as well as a genuine interest in learning. Once when one of his beer-sodden mates was about to heave a five-gallon drum at the nearest white person, who happened to be me, he calmly walked up to him, relieved the young man of his load, and told him to bugger off. I was impressed.

When the new teacher finally arrived I found myself without a job. I was no mechanic, accountant, or other specialist required to help the community function. I had a degree in anthropology with an emphasis on Australian Aboriginal studies, but it mostly dealt with traditional culture, not the demoralized and deracinated residue that typified contemporary Aboriginal society. However, a number of community elders could still remember life before the mission and were keen to pass on that memory to the younger generation. When it was suggested I work with them, I gladly accepted. I was now the pupil, not the teacher. I watched and listened as the old people carved didgeridoos and boab nuts, taught me 'language', or took me out bush to hunt and show me survival skills. It was a rare and precious moment in my life.

My stay in this community was cut short by a request in late 1976 to go to India. As the Maharashtra Village Development Project expanded from one pilot village it needed foreign staff trained in the Institute's participatory methods to work with young Indian trainees. Our job was to conduct planning consultations in villages that had elected to be part of the scheme, then live and work in those communities to help them put their plans into practice. It sounded like a mathematical formula that, if followed, would produce the desired results. The reality was somewhat different.

With devastating cycles of dysentery, endless bus and train travel, and living on a frugal village diet my body began to show the strain. I lost a lot of weight but when I fell asleep in a staff meeting I realized I'd reached my limits. In addition, our fundraising was failing to keep up with our ever-growing needs. When I spent my last rupee in one village to pay off our debt to a shopkeeper, it was humiliating to say the least. We claimed to be promoting economic self-sufficiency and social self-reliance and couldn't support our own staff on a bare-bones budget. The gap between story and reality became increasingly untenable, so I requested to return to Australia and vowed never to return to India.

But once it has you in its clutches India does not readily let you go. Less than two years later I was back, although in quite different circumstances. I had accumulated a modest cash reserve, had a permanent city residence instead of an ever-changing string of village abodes, and diverse food and medical care were within easy reach. I was part of a Bombay-based team to raise funds for our village work. Instead of riding buses from village to village I now traveled by train from city to city. It was like a lateral promotion. Along with Indian colleagues I visited cities across the country, meeting India's business leaders, representatives of foreign governments, and others. One year I covered more than 40,000 kilometers by rail. Train journeys introduced me to people from all walks of life and were the beginning of many friendships.

This second stint in India (1980-1984) was the most transformative time of my life. During this period the Institute became the organizing sponsor of a vast global undertaking called the International Exposition of Rural Development (IERD). Spread over three years, the IERD brought together representatives of NGOs, governments, private companies, donor agencies and grassroots communities engaged in helping the world's poor pull themselves out of poverty. The theme, Sharing Approaches That Work, accented breakthroughs and replicable models. The centerpiece of the IERD was a 10-day event in India, beginning and ending in New Delhi and involving 35 host projects across the country. Many attendees had never been on a plane or possessed a passport. For our team, it added a new layer to our work as we secured sponsorship and funding in India and abroad. For me, it meant more traveling, meeting more people in higher echelons of society, and playing more conspicuous and weighty public roles. It was exhilarating and exhausting.

During these four years something even more dramatic and redefining happened to me. I was in my young 30s and after two abortive attempts to marry, still single. All my adult life I had lived in community and had most of my basic needs taken care of. But India triggered something deep inside me I had long repressed. In India men are prominent in public life and a high percentage seems blessed with good looks. Also, it is acceptable for young males to show affection for one another in public, in contrast to the macho Australia in which I grew up. These two things finally wore me down. After chancing upon a magazine article on the subject I decided to 'explore my gay potential'. Once I had crossed the line there was no turning back. I discovered an entire part of myself I never knew existed, albeit in a society in which homosexuality was illegal. The next few years were a roller coaster of untold highs and life-threatening lows. My memoir, *The Boatman*, published 30 years later, chronicles this experience.

* * *

I left India reluctantly in 1984. Had I stayed, I almost certainly would have succumbed to AIDS, which had recently arrived and about which very little was known. Had it not been for gay colleagues in the US who sent me information on the subject I would have been none the wiser. That I had gay colleagues was itself a revelation that occurred during my last year in India. Once we began to connect and become known a surprising number of LGBT staff joined our ranks. We published a talking paper on homosexuality and the role of gay people in the Institute, where traditional heterosexual families had been the norm, particularly in leadership roles. We used an all-staff gathering in Chicago in 1984 to present our case and found widespread support.

Although India still tugged at my heartstrings, I found myself drawn in another direction. Building on my fundraising experience, I was asked to join our Brussels-based International Development and Funding (IDF) team to raise money and other resources to assist field staff in various countries. Visits to government agencies, UN offices and private funding bodies became standard fare. European trains were a lot smoother and more comfortable than those in India but they lacked the vibrant human exchange I'd come to know and love. No-one shared their home cooking with me, invited me to their family restaurant, or tried to marry me to their daughter.

Over the next four years I traveled extensively to other parts of the world, especially Africa and Asia, to help secure grants, represent our secretariat at staff meetings, and liaise with other NGOs. I began to piggyback excursions on to my official agenda, thanks to the goodwill and kindness of colleagues and local people. I came to regard these 'add-ons' as more rewarding than my actual work. After each trip I would write about my experiences to family and friends; a number of those letters form the basis of stories in this collection.

My time in Brussels flew by. Europe's close-knit yet culturally-diverse nature was intoxicating. Going to a local pub and hearing multiple languages spoken made me want to master more than my university French and high-school German. Witnessing ancient festivals reenacted in neighborhood plazas made me realize how limited my sense of history was. And hosting colleagues and visitors from all over Europe and around the world gave me a sense of being at the center of things for the first time in my life.

Brussels was important to me for two reasons. The Institute had contracted with a German publisher to produce a trilogy of books about the IERD. Two had been completed but when the person in charge of the project left Brussels it raised the question who would take responsibility for the third, which was to document what we had learned from this undertaking. I volunteered, albeit with no experience of editing or of this new-fangled thing called desktop publishing. After a steep learning curve and numerous extended deadlines I produced my first book, *Approaches That Work in Rural Development*. It was not the most profound or gripping tome but it reignited my love of words and set me on a path that has continued to this day.

Our IDF team budgeted a small amount for 'self-improvement' for its members, so I chose to do a correspondence course in creative writing from London. By the time I completed the course three years later I was able to place every piece I wrote in a variety of publications. I was hesitant to call myself a writer but I was on a new trajectory, even though its ultimate destination was far from clear.

Another thing that happened during my four years in Brussels was equally, if not more, significant. After exploring my new-found sexual identity in India, I'd come to feel more comfortable as a gay man. I was in my young 30s and began to contemplate a committed relationship for the first time. But my initial attempt was not satisfying and left me wondering if I was destined to live a solitary life. Then I heard of an American colleague who was divorcing. Rumor had it he was gay. I wasn't sure what to make of this but penned him a letter and waited to see what would happen.

Bruce's welcoming reply was the first of dozens of letters and tapes we exchanged over the next two years. During that time we met just twice before deciding to create a new family that included his two young children and their mother. Some warned against such a move; others thought us crazy. We had very little money, few prospects for employment, and near impossible hurdles to clear so I could emigrate to the US. The Institute was morphing from a social movement to a more traditional NGO and offered me a 'job' in Seattle. On 14th October 1988 I boarded a plane in Brussels and arrived in Seattle on a rainy Friday evening to begin my life in a new country, with a new job and a new family.

In the ensuing years I continued to travel as part of my work, as well as for pleasure, adding personal excursions to work trips and conferences. In December 2000 I resigned from the ICA to focus on personal writing and undertake a transition from city resident to island dweller. This ended a 30-year association with the Institute that had taken me to many corners of the earth, pushed me to operate outside my comfort zone, and equipped me with a range of skills I might otherwise not have acquired.

Around the same time Bruce made the leap from psychotherapist to flight attendant. Although fraught with challenges, his new job afforded us highly discounted travel, allowing us to visit places as varied as Tasmania and Tierra del Fuego, Mexico and Meghalaya. Wherever we go, we try to educate ourselves about the culture and history, learn some local language, and link up with people who can provide insights to the region. In contrast to my younger days when

I'd let fate whisk me off to exotic locations, we seek to strike a balance between preparing ourselves and going with flow.

As I've aged my passion for exploring the world has not abated. If anything, it has increased. But having a traveling companion has made it more pleasant and reassuring. We favor similar activities, delight in discovering different cuisines, and enjoy making new friends. Bruce counters my always-on-the-go propensity with a just-stay-put approach. And our history with the Institute not only connects us to an extensive network of caring and talented people but provides us with a set of core values and common perspectives that infuse whatever we do. I count myself fortunate to have been given such gifts and hope this collection of stories will allow others to share in them.

WELCOME TO THE USA

· · · · ·

Arriving in a new country for the first time is often intimidating, no matter how familiar you may be with the procedure. Even after more than 40 entries I find myself on edge. But one arrival stands out above all others.

My first trip abroad was to the United States in October 1971. I had just celebrated my 22nd birthday and decided to take a quantum leap from suburban Perth, Western Australia to Chicago's West Side, a black ghetto. It's hard to imagine two places more contrasting but I was young, naïve and ready to take on the world, albeit terrified at what might await me. Before I left a colleague who had made the same journey pulled me aside. "America can be overwhelming and some Australians react defensively. Don't make that mistake. Just be yourself, take things in your stride, and remember to laugh."

Flying from Perth to Chicago was no simple affair nearly 50 years ago. It involved stops in Sydney, Suva, Honolulu, San

Francisco and New York. I left Perth on a Thursday night, spent a day in Sydney and arrived in Chicago on a Saturday afternoon. Being new to international travel, I lapped up every perk Qantas offered. Every movie they screened, I watched; every glass of wine they poured, I gulped down; every meal they served, I ate to the last crumb. By the time the champagne-and-lobster breakfast rolled around between Honolulu and San Francisco, I was feeling significantly heavier than when I left Perth. My body rhythms were shot and my digestive tract didn't know what had hit it.

My first taste of America was Hawaii. After flying for hours through pitch darkness I was shocked to look out the window and see a blaze of lights. As the captain announced preparations for landing, my stomach squirmed. Although I'd lived and worked with Americans in Australia, now I was about to meet them on their home turf. I'd rehearsed my story dozens of times: I was coming to the United States to do a six-month training program, after which I would return to Australia. Along with my non-immigrant visa, I had a letter of invitation from the Ecumenical Institute. Alles in Ordnung.

As we touched down in Honolulu I took a deep breath and tried to calm my nerves. We all had to go through immigration and customs so I was consoled by being one of a crowd submitting to the same fate. This was America, the land of dreams and possibility. But it was 1971. It was also the land of the civil rights movement, political assassinations, the Muslim Brotherhood, the Kent State University massacre and the Vietnam War. I had mixed feelings as I walked across the tarmac and entered the coach that ferried us to the immigration building.

My attempt to mingle with the crowd was somewhat thwarted by my attire — an orangey-brown woolen suit with flared pants coupled with a turquoise floral shirt and matching tie that made me look like a walking neon sign. A birthday gift from my mother, this outfit was pretty cutting-edge for its time, at least in tame old Perth. Even if I was a quivering mass of jelly inside, my state-of-the-art wardrobe was a useful disguise. Besides, the suit took up so much room in my case I had little choice but to wear it.

As I stood at the yellow line waiting to present my credentials, perspiration trickled down my armpits. I looked at the middle-aged man behind the counter. What was he like? Did he have a wife, two kids and a dog? Did he ever travel to other countries and have to go through this ordeal? What questions would he ask? Would he trigger my propensity to stutter under stress? When the woman before me picked up her bag and moved on, the officer uttered a long, almost bored "n-e-x-t". I strode up to the counter and pushed my passport and immigration card under the glass. Flicking open the passport, he stared at the visa for an interminable time, then glanced at me with a stern, uncompromising stare.

"What's your purpose in coming to the United States?" he drawled.

"I, I, I'm coming for an international training program," I stammered.

"What kind of training?"

"Cultural studies."

"What organization is this with?"

"The E-e-e-ecumenical Institute."

"Where's this institute?"

"Chicago."

"How long is the course?"

"Six months."

Then I remembered the letter of invitation from the Institute. Damn! I'd left it on the plane. How could I have been so bloody stupid?

"This isn't the right kind of visa for a six-month training program. It's only valid for three months," said the officer.

I nearly melted on the spot. My armpits were like the Mississippi in flood. I had to do something. In the game we were playing it was clear I was on the losing side.

"The US Consulate in Perth gave me this visa for the training program. And I have a letter from the Institute but I left it on the plane, sir."

I decided to add the most unAustralian 'sir' in the vain hope it might improve my position, which appeared to be getting weaker every word I uttered. Instead it only seemed to make matters worse.

"I'll have you know, young man, that I decide who enters the United States, not some consular officer."

I began to visualize myself being led handcuffed to the next plane back to Sydney. While I stood contemplating my fate, the officer consulted with a colleague. This didn't look good. Minutes ticked by. I was fast needing to find a toilet. Then he returned, grabbed a piece of paper, and slid it through the opening.

"I'll let you through this time but when you get to Chicago you'll need to take this to the INS office and get a three-month extension."

He picked up his rubber stamp, belted it down on the page, and shoved my passport back with the same indifference with which he'd greeted me.

"Thank you…sir," I replied meekly, and beat a hasty retreat to the door marked Transit Lounge.

Although I had advised the Institute's office in San Francisco of my arrival, I wasn't sure they had received the letter, so I decided to send a telegram. This meant changing the precious $50 bill my father had given me at Perth airport. Fortunately, the exchange rate was in my favor but when I learned what the telegram would cost I had second thoughts. However, I wanted to make the most of my six-hour layover in this famous city and knowing someone would meet me was reassuring, so I sent it.

∗ ∗ ∗

On 25th October 1971 the United Nations voted to accept the People's Republic of China in place of Taiwan. Its Communist government under the leadership of Mao Tse Tung had come to power in October 1949, two weeks after I was born. How odd, I thought. It was as though China and I had grown up together, albeit worlds apart. It was finally making its debut on the world stage as I was launching mine. It would be several months before President Nixon would make his historic trip to China, but in the meantime another American upstaged him.

Huey Newton was the 29 year-old African-American leader of the Black Panther Party, which believed in worldwide revolution. Imagine the Panthers' delight when they received an invitation for Newton to visit the People's Republic. His return to the US was eagerly awaited, so a press conference was arranged at San Francisco airport. Since there were no direct flights between China and the US mainland he had to fly via Hawaii, where it was thought he had joined our flight.

I knew nothing of this when I stepped outside the cabin door. I was relieved to have made it to the western shores of America and eagerly anticipated the break from flying. The key would be connecting with the person I hoped had come to meet me among the multitudes who greeted this flight. I had pinned the Institute's symbol — a thumbnail-size wedge blade — on my lapel but how anyone could see this at a distance I can't imagine. Prior to deplaning the captain announced that we would all be taken to a hotel during the layover in San Francisco. It didn't sound optional.

Before I could think of a way around this we were ushered into the terminal. Entering the airport lounge was like disappearing into a long tunnel. Lined up with military precision for 30 meters on either side of me were black men and women, some with afro hairstyles and all dressed in black. I had known Aboriginal people in Australia but these were nothing like them. They had an intensity and intentionality I'd never encountered. They looked straight ahead, unblinking, feet apart and arms by their sides. I had read about the civil rights movement, I had reviewed *The Autobiography of Malcolm X*, and I had seen television programs about 'black is beautiful', but nothing prepared me for this.

At the end of this elaborate guard of honor was a frenzied mob of television crews, newspaper reporters and radio broadcasters. I felt I was wandering around in a film set where I had no right to be. Adding to this surreal sense was the large number of police trying to keep the surging crowd at bay. But these weren't like Australian police. They were armed and ready for action. But why all this hoopla? Was this how all overseas flights to the US were met?

Although I didn't know it, my telegram had made it to our San Francisco office, which dispatched Jann McGuire to meet me. Unfortunately, Jann had no idea what I looked like. Given the mayhem at the airport she might well have given up in despair and returned home. But not Jann. Nearly 50 years later she remembers that night clearly.

"The entire Black Panther Party was at the airport to meet Huey Newton, marching in formation in their black berets. Airport security was a little panicked and sent John's Qantas plane to an obscure runway and gate, and since I didn't know him I had a hard time connecting with him. I walked up to many people when I finally found where the passengers had come in from his plane, yelling 'Mr. Burbidge?'"

Alas, I never heard Jann's desperate calls. I frantically scanned the crowd for someone who appeared to be looking for me, but saw no-one. Meanwhile, the Qantas crew was determined to get us out of there and into a bus as quickly as possible. I tried to convince a flight attendant I needed to leave the group, but she wouldn't hear of it. We were whisked out of the airport and half an hour later found ourselves in a hotel, where we were herded into the restaurant for yet another meal. The last thing I needed was more food, but I dutifully joined another passenger and proceeded to order.

Just as I was starting my seafood cocktail, a tallish young woman with blond hair entered the restaurant. She stood for a moment and surveyed the crowd before buttonholing a waiter, who then asked the entire room, "Is there a Mr. Burbridge here?" Forgiving his mispronunciation of my name, I dropped my spoon and raised my hand. The woman came over to my table and introduced herself. As I recall the moment, I think of the movie title *An Angel At My Table*. Jann had appeared from nowhere and I'd swear she had wings. We exchanged a few pleasantries and she recounted how she had searched for me in vain at the airport. When that failed she persisted with the Qantas staff until they disclosed where they had taken us. But time was short. Would I like to go to see some of the city and visit the Institute? I was delighted to accept her offer, so excused myself and told my fellow passenger I'd meet her back at the airport in a few hours.

When the airline staff counted New York-bound passengers for the return trip to the airport they were one short. A quick scan of the passenger manifesto revealed that I was the culprit. My traveling companion hadn't told them I had left with a friend, so the crew were beside themselves. Who was this scoundrel who had vanished into the San Francisco night without permission? While Qantas was about to issue a missing persons alert, I was blissfully enjoying my first tour of an American city. I don't recall much of those few hours but I do remember the dressing-down I received at the airport on my return.

"Where the hell do you think you've been young man?" said an irate ticketing agent who looked like she was about to devour me on the spot.

"We've been searching everywhere for you. We were about to call the police. You just disappeared from the restaurant without telling us!"

I felt like the errant schoolboy who had broken the most hallowed school rule. It was all I could do to make brief eye contact. Somehow I managed to muster an apology, but to little effect.

"You had no right to run off like that without our permission," she snapped.

Wracked with guilt, I took the ticket she thrust toward me and headed for the plane. I still had to cross this vast continent and catch another flight to Chicago. I had no idea that the final leg of this journey would present challenges of a whole different order.

* * *

Chicago. A mythical place in my imagination, probably due to my watching too many episodes of *The Untouchables*, as much as anything. There was also the urban sociology class I took at university, in which Chicago was heralded as the living laboratory of the modern city, with its highly distinctive ethnic enclaves. But it was the story of Fifth City, the Institute's community revitalization project on the city's destitute West Side, that hooked me.

This grassroots effort to change the fortunes of the impoverished black population who lived in a 20-block area was unlike most other 1960s attempts at urban renewal. Spearheaded by a core of Institute staff who lived in an abandoned seminary in the ghetto, the project aimed to transform the imagination of the local residents from being hapless victims of uncontrollable forces to masters of their own destiny. This was done in myriad ways from operating a community-run preschool to creating small businesses such as a laundromat and grocery store, opening a health clinic and remodeling derelict housing. The premise was, if you could do it here you could it anywhere.

After I said good-bye to my beloved Qantas crew in New York and found the American Airlines plane to Chicago it seemed all downhill. When the captain announced we had begun our descent, I tried to gird myself for my entry into this strange place that would be my home for the next six months. Till now I had cocooned myself in the unreal world of air travel, but that was about to end and there was no turning back.

As our Boeing-707 prepared to land, I peered out the window. My first image of this massive metropolis was gigantic tank stands thrusting up from a pancake-flat landscape. As the plane slowly turned in a 180-degree arc I glimpsed the soaring towers of downtown Chicago in the distance. As we grew closer to the ground I noticed the trees had no foliage, as if someone had taken a giant vacuum cleaner and sucked up every leaf. I was seeing my first fall landscape but it wasn't anything like the brilliant calendar images of a North American autumn.

Upon arrival at the airport I made straight for the luggage carousel. The last time I had seen my case was in Honolulu, which seemed light years ago. Did it make it to San Francisco and New York to Chicago? Given all I'd been through I was expecting the worst. Finally, after all the luggage had completed several circuits, out it slid through the rubber slats. I breathed a sigh of relief.

From the airport I had been instructed to go to the downtown Palmer House hotel, from where I would take a taxi to the Institute's campus. I found the bus but was aghast how many of my new dollars the ride cost. Most of the journey was on freeways surging with traffic at speeds I'd never encountered. When the bus pulled up outside the stately Palmer House a doorman offered to carry my case inside, but I indicated I needed a taxi instead. Several cabs were lined up outside the hotel, so I went to the head of the line. The young driver jumped out to greet me and asked my destination. I had seen the address so many times it was etched in my memory.

"3444 West Congress Parkway," I announced proudly.

The driver screwed up his eyes and gave me a weird look.

"You sure you have that right, buddy?" he asked.

"Oh yes," I replied. "It's the Ecumenical Institute," as though that should have removed any doubt.

"Economical Institute?" he queried. "Never heard of it."

Not be outdone, I pulled out the invitation letter I had been sent by the Institute. The driver stared at it as though it were written in Chinese.

"Sorry pal, don't know it," he said. "Try the next guy."

I picked up my case and trudged to the next cab. The driver was African American. This should do the trick, I thought. After all, the part of the West Side I wanted to go to was almost totally black. The driver didn't bother to get out of the cab but lent over to the passenger side.

"Where ya headin?" he asked between chewing gum.

"The West Side. 3444 West Congress Parkway. Between the Kedzie and Homan exits."

I was sure the extra detail would seal the deal. At least it would show that I knew what I was talking about.

"Are you crazy?" he asked as he rolled his eyes skyward. "You'd never get me to go there if you paid three times the fare."

I couldn't believe it. I'd come more than half way round the world, I'd finally got within spitting distance of my destination, and I couldn't get a black taxi driver to take me to the black ghetto!

With a heavy heart, I started towards the next cab while repeating the old maxim, third time lucky. As I did, a doorman from the hotel came striding over.

"Can I help you, sir?" he asked politely.

"I sure hope you can," I replied more curtly than I intended. "I'm trying to get to this address," I said, as I thrust the invitation letter under his nose. "But these guys say they don't know it or won't go there."

He looked at the letterhead and frowned.

"Hmm, I can see why you might be having a little problem," he said. "This ain't the nicest part of town. But let me see what I can do."

Waving me to follow, he went to the third cab and spoke with the young black driver. After a brief discussion the driver opened his door and made for the rear of the car. I walked towards him and offered him my case, which he dumped unceremoniously in the trunk.

"Hop in," he yelled.

I barely had time to thank the doorman for his assistance, let alone offer him a tip, although my limited resources and Australian antipathy to tipping curbed that. However, another Australian custom I assiduously avoided. Instead of jumping in the front seat and chatting with the driver, I slid into the back and held my breath.

The car sped away from sidewalk into thick traffic. Within minutes we were heading west down the Eisenhower Expressway. The only freeway I had known was nothing like this — the sheer number of cars, their excessive size, and the speed at which they tore past were unnerving. It was like being in a mob of bumper cars that were hurtling out of control and might crash any moment. The freeway was below the surrounding neighborhoods so I had to look up to see the passing view. For the most part it was endless rows of three-story houses, all the same gray wooden constructions. The absence of color was depressing.

As we zipped past exits I tried to capture their names on the overhead signs. When I saw Kedzie I looked to see if the driver noticed it but he didn't seem to. Did he know where he was going? Was he taking me on a joy ride to extend the fare? Then I noticed a sign for the Homan exit. The driver changed lanes and edged over to the off-ramp, before pulling off the freeway and decelerating. We cruised around the neighborhood searching for our destination but saw only boarded-up buildings and empty lots strewn with appliances and abandoned cars.

"What's this place called yer lookin for?" asked the driver.

"It's the Ecu-men-ical Institute," I replied, as if giving elocution lessons.

"Wazzat? Some kind of school or what?"

"Yeah, like a college," I said, although I had no idea what the Institute campus looked like.

He swerved over to the sidewalk and pulled up beside three young black men who eyed us suspiciously.

"You know some Institute around here?" the driver asked.

The older-looking one among them stepped forward.

"Yeah."

"Yeah, what?" said the driver.

"Two blocks down and hang a left."

The driver sped off and within minutes we drew up alongside an imposing stone building set in a large quadrangle, surrounded by a high fence and with a church spire in the background. I scanned the building for an entrance, but nothing stood out. Then I spotted a door with an armed guard outside.

"Stop here," I instructed the driver.

As the car slid over to the curb, the guard ambled towards us. I looked at the meter and gulped. My American dollars were rapidly disappearing. I counted out the amount on the meter and put it in my pocket. The driver went to the trunk and hauled out my case. I handed him the money. He checked each bill and scowled.

"No tip?" he asked.

"Sorry mate, that's all I've got," I pretended in my best Australian accent.

The security guard didn't seem impressed with my generosity either, but he let it pass.

"You lookin for the Ecoomenical Institoot?" he queried.

"Yes, I am," I replied, relieved that at last I had found someone who knew what I was talking about.

He pointed to the door. As he did, I noticed a tarnished brass plaque that was invisible from the road. So this was the grand establishment, as nondescript as you would expect the headquarters of such a nondescript organization to be.

I took a deep breath and rallied myself one last time. When I reached the door, I gave it a sharp rap. No response. I tried again and looked at the guard.

"Sometimes it takes a few minutes if the person on dooty isn't there," he remarked.

I waited then knocked a third time. The door opened and a tall young man with sharp black eyes and a balding head appeared, walkie-talkie in his left hand.

"Hi, I said. I'm John Burbidge. I've come from Australia. I'm here for the Global Academy."

"C-c-c-c-ome inside. I'm H-H-H-H-Henry S-S-S-S-Seale," he stuttered, as he held out his right hand to greet me.

Henry's speech impediment seemed much worse than mine, which I managed to conceal most of the time. In a strange way it was reassuring to find another person in the Institute who shared my little secret. What were the odds, I wondered, out of hundreds of staff that the first person I should meet was someone who also stuttered. Henry never would have guessed how strangely comforting this was to me.

As I entered the building I began to relax slightly. It was more than three days since I'd left Perth but it seemed a lot longer. I was exhausted, but had finally made it.

Welcome to the United States of America, I said silently to myself.

KING OF THE ROAD

. . . . .

Two weeks before, I had no idea I'd be going to Africa. When it was suggested that I might represent our Brussels-based secretariat at a meeting of our Africa staff in Zambia, I had serious reservations. My previous trip to Africa ten years before (see *Ambassadors at Large*) had left bitter memories. When I arrived in Zambia in January 1986 and discovered we were meeting in the same compound as the outlawed African National Congress (ANC), Swaziland union leaders and Ugandan refugees, I grew more concerned. Armed guards at the gate and floodlights around the perimeter of the compound reminded me that we were in a volatile part of the world. While we were meeting, three coup d'états occurred in the region and a letter bomb exploded in the ANC's Lusaka post office box. As we listened to reports about our work to help villagers lift their communities out of poverty, the continent seemed to be erupting around us.

After the meeting I had a week before returning to Brussels so I decided to acquaint myself more with this part of the world. Since I had no vehicle and public transport was minimal, I chose to hitchhike. My colleagues, both foreign and Zambian, did it all the time and assured me it was safe. My first hitch was in the back of a battered pick-up in drizzling rain on the road to Victoria Falls. The vehicle's hood kept unlocking so every few kilometers the driver would stop to batten it down, while I slunk further down under my umbrella. When he dropped me at Monze 180 kilometers southwest of Lusaka, I thanked him and looked around the hotel parking lot for other options.

At that moment, a silver Toyota Cressida sedan pulled up nearby. It looked as though it had just been driven off the sale lot. I strode over to the car and approached the two safari-suited African men sitting in front.

"You guys going to Livingstone?" I inquired.

"Sure. Want a lift?"

Before I could answer they had got out of the car and beckoned me to join them as they headed for the bar. After we'd downed a couple of beers we returned to the car and they ushered me into the back seat, where the vehicle's factory-fresh scent washed over me. With its air-conditioning, wooden trim and digital instrument panel I wondered how my companions could have afforded such a luxurious car, but my thoughts were drowned out by the disco music blaring through the twin speakers behind my head. Between changing tapes we chatted and exchanged business cards. The embossed gold lettering on theirs said they were in the freight business, but something told me I'd be wise not to ask what kind of freight. A crocodile skin-covered briefcase lying next to me in the back seat was unnerving enough.

For most of our journey I kept silent and occasionally dozed, but when the car slowed and turned off the road onto a dirt track my anxiety level shot up. Several days before an Indian doctor and his children had been held at gunpoint and forced to strip naked as attackers robbed them. When the car came to a halt I was ready to run. My companions jumped out of the car and told me to do the same. One of them flung open the trunk and reached for a bag in the corner. I glanced around. The area toward the road offered no cover and the opposite direction was little better. As I frantically tried to figure out an escape route, the driver grabbed the bag and unzipped it. He reached in and pulled out something. I held my breath. Then he turned and faced me, his right hand gripping a bottle of Johnny Walker Black Label.

"Hey, young fella. Like a little drink? Gotta be careful round here. Don't want to get nabbed by the police. They'll rip off your liquor and slap a fine on you."

He produced a plastic cup and offered it to me half full while he and his partner shared the bottle between them. First beer, now whiskey, and premium imported whiskey at that. It was mid-afternoon and I hadn't eaten since early morning. I dislike drinking on an empty stomach, but had little choice. After they'd had their fill the driver stashed away the bottle and we resumed our journey. He kept his foot firmly on the accelerator while I prayed we'd make it safely to Livingstone. We arrived less than five hours after I'd left Lusaka, with two stops. I later learned this was unheard of.

* * *

I didn't know it then but this and another hitch to Zambia's Copperbelt were preparing me for my third and most rewarding adventure. I'd heard that Zimbabwe, in stark contrast to Zambia, was then one of Africa's economic success stories, so I decided to check it out. My journey began at an agricultural research station on the outskirts of Lusaka as the guest of an American family who were friends of our project staff. They offered to put me up overnight so I could get an early start the following day.

Next morning I made my way out of the research station around 7:30 and walked to the other side of the two-lane road that linked Lusaka to Harare 400 kilometers away. It had rained lightly overnight so the red earth gave off a fresh, soothing scent. Although the sun was well up by now the cool air tempered its effect. I donned my broad-brimmed canvas hat, placed my overnight bag near the side of the road with a 'Harare' sign on top, and sat back under a poinciana tree.

One of my colleagues had explained to me the rules of hitchhiking in Africa. Unlike other parts of the world, thumbing a ride here could be taken as offensive. Instead, you created a sign with the name of your destination, placed it on your luggage at the roadside, and waited nearby. When a vehicle approached you waved your arm up and down, palm open and facing the ground.

Traffic was light. A few small cars and the odd pick-up scuttled by, but none stopped. More vehicles seemed to be coming into Lusaka than leaving it. After more than an hour I began to wonder how long I might have to wait. Every time a truck approached I leaped up expectantly, only to have my hopes dashed as it went sailing past. By 9:00 o'clock I was having second thoughts about this venture. I hadn't had difficulty getting rides before. Was Harare the problem or had I just struck one of those days?

Nearly two hours lapsed, the temperature was rising, and my spirits were flagging. I was walking up and down to stretch my legs when I heard the groan of changing gears and the hiss of power breaks. I turned around to see an enormous blue and white Scania truck slowing down and coming to a halt just a few meters from my luggage. I raced back, grabbed my bag, and ran to the driver's side of the cab where a sunburned arm hung out the window.

"Wanna ride to Harare, mate? Hop in."

The words had a magical ring. I didn't expect to find someone going all the way to Harare. I ran around to the passenger side, hoisted myself up the giant steps, and plunked down in the cabin. It was huge with an area behind the seat large enough to lie down in.

"Throw your gear back there," said the driver with a toss of his head. Then, turning partly in my direction, he stretched out his hairy arm, palm open.

"John Denby's the name. Call me JD."

"Well, I guess that makes me JB then," I said, introducing myself.

"Been waitin' long?"

"A couple of hours."

"Where ya from?"

"Well, originally Australia, but I live in Brussels."

"A Brussel sprout, eh? I thought I detected a little Oz there somewhere. I spent a few years there meself some time back. Did a bit of farming in New South Wales. After I'd had a couple of years working in New Zealand and before I moved to Rhodesia."

I felt like I was tracking a moving target.

"So what part of the old country are you from?" I asked.

"Yorkshire, mate. Left home when I was 19. Seems like ages ago. Young and naïve I was. Couldn't wait to get away. Didn't really matter where, just had to go."

"Interesting. I took off when I was just a bit older than you. Went to Chicago for a year, then Toronto and Ottawa for a couple of years, back to Australia, then to India and now Belgium."

Our tit-for-tat game took on a tone of friendly one-upmanship. Without realizing it we had set ourselves up for a five-hour conversation. Each had questions of the other and stories sparked more stories. We roamed from the Chicago ghetto to the Zimbabwean war of independence, from a remote Aboriginal community in northwestern Australia to a tobacco farm in former Rhodesia. There seemed no end to our meandering tales.

Dressed in little black shorts with his beer-gut belly spilling over, JD sat commanding his $150,000 behemoth like a man who had found his calling. I couldn't get Roger Miller's *King of the Road* out of my mind, although JD was in better financial circumstances than that song's legendary character. He let drop that he earned about US$9,000 a month on trips between southern and eastern Africa. When the war came in the 1970s he decided to swap farming for the road. It was a lonely job but several times a month he passed through Harare where he spent time with his family.

"So what brought you to this part of the world?" asked JD.

I told him my story, including my recent travels throughout Zambia.

"Well, I'll be damned," he said. "I reckon I picked up a couple of your mates this morning on the other side of Lusaka. Dropped them off in town just half an hour ago. He was pretty quiet but she kinda made up for him. Living in a village, they said. Some place starting with a K."

"What a coincidence!" I said. "That's them all right. John and Elaine Telford. From Kapini."

JD chuckled and mumbled something about the smallness of the world. What were the chances of us both hitching a ride on the same day with the same trucker? It was the first of several occurrences that made me feel I was meant to meet JD. It was as though he was the reason I had come to Africa.

Conversation flowed so freely that I was surprised how quickly we reached Kafue, where the road forks southwest to Namibia and Botswana and southeast to Harare. A few kilometers out of town we crossed the slow-flowing Kafue River on its way to join the mighty Zambezi in the valley below. JD thrust the truck into low gear as we began our descent, gradual at first but increasingly steep as we exchanged the cool air of the escarpment for the steamier lower reaches of the river valley.

I sat stunned at the yawning vista that opened up before me. There is something about an expansive view that stretches the mind. I felt I was in that small plane in the movie *Out of Africa*, surveying the grandeur of the terrain below. The word 'awe' must have been invented for moments like this. We didn't talk much as we descended towards the border crossing at Chirundu. JD had to give all his attention to controlling the truck, while I sat mesmerized by the brilliant tapestry unfolding before us.

I was jolted out of my reverie as the truck came to a jarring halt in a long line of vehicles at the Zimbabwe border post. JD pointed me in the direction of immigration control while he headed to the customs building. I joined the queue and gritted my teeth for a long wait but was surprised how quickly it moved. I anticipated having to grease palms but it never happened. Was Zimbabwe an exception to the rule? But as if to make up for it, several monkeys scampered across my path and looked up at me expectantly.

From what little I'd seen Chirundu didn't offer many enticements. I later learned it was the home of Zambia's bustling sex industry, fueled by the constant flow of truck drivers and migratory agricultural workers. Girls as young as 12 offered their services, often in exchange for food or a bar of soap. Sadly, many would succumb to sexually transmitted diseases before they reached adulthood. Zambia had one of the world's highest incidences of AIDS, a fact that was confirmed for me when I learned that a major bank over-recruited management trainees because a percentage would succumb to the disease before they were ready to work.

But on that bright February morning such concerns eluded me. When JD returned we continued down the Cape-to-Cairo Road. Immediately we had crossed the Zambezi we began our slow climb up the escarpment. Black tire marks seared into the asphalt reminded me of the treachery of this major African artery. I held my breath as JD maneuvered the truck to within centimeters of the gravel verge, from which the hillside dropped sharply to the valley floor far below. Although his concentration never faltered, this didn't deter him from giving a running commentary as we ground our way up the slope.

"Over to ya left there about 80 kilometers is Mana Pools National Park. Some nice camping spots. Good fishing too. During the dry season you'll see all kinds of animals coming down to drink...hey, what's that over there?

"Where?" I said, trying to follow his jutting chin.

"Near that clump of bushes. I'd say it's probably baboons. Yep, tis. Sure as eggs."

I spotted them. My first sighting of animals in the wild in Africa made me thirst for more. From then on I kept my eyes glued on the passing landscape and was amply rewarded. Before we had gone far we spotted elephants, impala and water buffalo. I was on safari and not paying a cent for it.

"Used to see lions and leopards once in a while, but they're a rare sight these days. Especially since the Bush War."

"Tell me about the war. What was it like? What part did you play in it?"

His eyes glazed over as he seemed to retreat into another world. With one hand on the wheel, he would gesture with the other. Pointing to a low ridge in the distance he said, "That's where we pushed the rebel forces back into Zambia." And a short while later, "See that hill over there. We took that after a three-day battle. Lost several men. They lost a whole lot more."

I discovered that 'we' were the Rhodesian Security Forces with whom Denby, then a landowning farmer, had thrown in his lot in the name of survival. 'They' were either of the two main guerilla forces, which represented a black population that outnumbered the white 22 to 1. Their protracted war lasted 15 years but finally ended white minority-rule and the creation of the Republic of Zimbabwe.

"What was it like being on the losing side?"

"Not so bad really. Had to happen sooner or later. It's been six years now and things have settled down a bit. White and black get on a lot better here than in South Africa. We have a black servant family and I trust them with my life."

Who was this man I was sitting next to? Bit by bit, I began to put together the pieces of the puzzle that made up his life but I was a long way from finishing it. Just as I was about to probe a little deeper he interrupted me.

"Look. Over there. Those blokes with rifles slung over their backs. They're after rhino poachers from Zambia. Terrible waste. The poachers kill the animals just to get the horn. Six poachers were shot last week. Good riddance to them, I say."

Stories kept tumbling out of his mouth like water from an open tap. But one riveted me more than any other. It happened to JD two nights before in Dar es Salaam, Tanzania.

"I'd parked me truck outside a hotel by the ocean. I left the window down slightly to get a little breeze into the cab. Sleep better that way. I'd turned in for the night," he said, motioning with his head to the bunk behind him. "About one in the morning I woke up with a start to find a black face leering over me and a knife at my throat. Demanded all my valuables.

Could hardly bargain with him, could I? So I offloaded my watch, alarm clock, camera and wedding ring. At least I kept my throat intact and I still have me truck. I usually have my little dog with me but I didn't bring him this trip because he had to go to the vet. Just my damn luck."

JD's seeming nonchalance as he described this episode floored me. I racked my brains for something comforting to say but everything I thought of seemed so trite.

"Guess I was even luckier than I realized that you showed up this morning," I said. He chuckled and threw me a hint of a smile.

As we neared the top of the escarpment a giant baobab tree caught my eye. I was transported back to northwestern Australia where I'd lived in the mid-1970s. Boabs, as they are known there, are a feature of that ancient landscape, as they are in this part of Africa and Madagascar. This tree looked to be at least 15 meters tall and about 4 meters in diameter. Its bloated, water-carrying trunk gave it a grossly overweight look.

"You know JD, in Australia there's one boab that's so broad and hollow that some say it was used to lock up Aboriginal prisoners."

"You're kidding," he said, rolling his head from side to side in disbelief. "There's no telling what lengths some people will go to, is there?"

At that moment JD braked, slowed down, and pulled the truck over to the side of the road. I thought we were going to take in the view or relieve our bladders.

"Hop out," he said. "There's someone I'd like you to meet."

Meet? Here and now? It didn't seem possible. I got down and walked around to the other side of the truck. Near the edge of the road sat an old black man huddled under a brightly colored blanket, a small metal plate at his feet.

"Hullo you old rascal," said JD.

The man turned his face in JD's direction and waved his hand.

"So it's you again, eh. I thought I recognized the sound of your truck. What mischief have you been up to?"

JD went over to the old man, knelt down beside him, and handed him a brown paper bag. The man took it, thrust his hand inside, and smiled.

"So you remembered what I like. I was getting low on chocolate. Just as well you showed up when you did."

"Yeah, I expected you'd be running out soon, you old bastard. Hey, I've brought someone to meet you. All the way from Australia…no Belgium…well, kind of everywhere. Bit like me."

JD motioned to me to move closer and hold out my hand. It was then I realized the old man was blind. He grasped my hand and gave it a firm shake.

"You like my country?" he asked.

"Yes, very much. It reminds me a lot of parts of my own, especially with all these bottle trees."

"Ah, the bottle trees. You can keep the trees and give me the bottles."

JD and I both laughed. We carried on our banter for a few more minutes before JD gave the old man a firm pat on the back and bid him farewell.

"Got to be going. The wife's expecting me home for dinner. Take care, old man."

We climbed back up into the cab and JD tooted the horn a couple of times as we headed to Makuti. A signpost outside the town said Cape Town was 3000 kilometers south and Cairo more than twice that far north. Closer at hand was the famous Cloud's End Hotel, an aptly name colonial hangover. Tired after a hard day's hunting you could lie back in a wicker chair on its terrace restaurant, sip a G & T, and survey the unimpeded view of the Zambezi valley. I took JD's word for it and let my imagination do the rest.

Once we had cleared the summit the landscape began to open up like a giant carpet unfurled in front of us. The precipitous gorges of the Zambezi gave way to undulating hills and scrub. Overhead bleached-white clouds filled the sky like giant powder puffs. At times I wondered if I was back in Australia, where the vastness of the land reminded me of my insignificance in the grand scheme of things. Just as I was about to drift off into another realm JD chimed in.

"Up a little further you'll see the first farms. Another 40 or 50 kilometers are some of the finest soya bean, maize and tobacco fields you'll ever see."

At times I felt as if I was reading a tourist brochure, but with JD's interjections it made fascinating reading. As we approached Kanoi tall brick chimneys dotted the horizon.

"Tobacco-curing sheds," said JD, reading my thoughts.

Then after a pause, he asked. "Like biltong?"

"Biltong? What's that? Zimbabwean for Vegemite?"

"Well, not quite that bad, although it tastes a bit like it. You probably know it as jerky. Real good to chew, especially on the road. Place here in Kanoi makes it. Here, try a bit," he said, as he reached into a box next to him and produced a strip of leathery-looking beef. "The wife introduced me to it. She loves it. Like most Afrikaners."

As we neared the outskirts of Harare the light receded and JD's thoughts began to turn towards home.

"How long are ya planning to stay in Harare?" he asked.

"Just a day or two. I have to be back in Lusaka by Friday night to catch my flight."

"Where ya putting up?"

"Hadn't given it much thought. Probably a youth hostel or the YMCA."

"Why don't you stay with us? I'm heading back north in two days' time. You can come back with me."

It seemed too good to be true. I gratefully accepted his kind invitation, wondering what 'us' would be like.

Within half an hour we entered the outskirts of Harare. High-rise buildings in the distance told me I was about to leave one Africa and enter another. Jacaranda trees lined broad boulevards and grassy playing fields were filled with soccer grounds and cricket pitches. When we pulled into a semi-circular driveway in the leafy suburb of Marlborough I did a double take. Before me was a large, two-storey house with broad French windows above the main entrance. A tennis court and swimming pool were part of the estate also.

"Sure beats a youth hostel," I thought to myself.

As we lowered ourselves from the cab a bevy of children and a small wire-haired terrier ran to greet us. I stood back to allow JD to enjoy the moment. As he signaled me to follow him into the house a tall, fair-haired woman appeared at the front door. JD introduced me to her as his wife, Priscilla. As soon as she spoke I recognized her South African roots. She didn't seem the least surprised as she welcomed me into their spacious living room. I wondered how many times JD returned home with a stranger in tow. But I didn't feel a stranger for long. Within minutes a black woman appeared with a tray of cold beers and Cokes, which were passed around the group eager to hear about JD's latest trip.

"So what's news?" said Priscilla.

JD held up his left-hand and waited for someone to ask a question.

"You're not going to tell me you pawned your wedding ring," said Priscilla with a wry smile.

"I wouldn't call it pawn," said JD. "More like an unintended exchange."

With that he related the events of two nights ago as if they were just another hiccup in his mobile life. The younger ones wanted to know more details; his wife and servant were more reserved. They seemed to understand how lucky they were that JD was here to tell about his bizarre adventure. After dinner over cups of chicory-laden coffee I discovered why. Each woman had a story to tell that made my stomach tighten. During the war, Priscilla's father, sister-in-law and niece had been blown up in a land mine at their farm gate. She later learned that it was intended for her brother. Her sister and brother-in-law had been shot in their bed, so she and JD had taken in their daughter, along with their own three children and an adopted son. But lest I heard only one side of this tragedy, JD told me that the Rhodesian forces razed to the ground the village of their servant's family. No one survived.

I heard many stories like these during my short stay in Zimbabwe. Given the tremendous pain and suffering all sides had experienced few wanted to see it continue. In a continent where tribalism and colonialism have been at the root of much bloodshed and violence, Zimbabwe's experiment in multiracialism offered hope. Sadly that would fade in the years to follow, but thanks to people like John Denby its seeds had been planted.

Two days later, JD and I headed back to Lusaka. As we approached the Chirundu border crossing, JD slowed down the truck, reached into his leather bag and produced several tins of boot polish.

"Planning to polish your shoes?" I asked.

"Not mine, mate. Customs officials. They have a certain weakness for the stuff, shall we say."

Whiskey, maybe. Used Levis, perhaps. But boot polish! Of all the things you could bribe officials with I'd never have thought of this.

"Why boot polish?" I asked.

"Simple. Zambia no longer makes it. Luxury item, mate. They can't afford to import the raw materials to produce it."

With that masterstroke we avoided the long queue of weary bodies snaking its way out of the door of the customs office, where a two- or three-hour wait was normal. Whether my companion also paid 'push money' usually demanded at African border crossings I didn't care to ask. John Denby was an old pro at this game so I trusted him implicitly.

Within 40 minutes we had cleared customs and immigration and were on our way. Sitting high up in the cab of his mighty Scania we quickly lapsed into more story telling. Our time together was coming to a close and we both wanted to make the most of it. Nearing the outskirts of Lusaka he said something that left me speechless.

"Ya know, we need more people who can transcend national and racial barriers. Global citizens I guess you'd call them."

If anyone embodied that phrase, it was John Denby.

Long after I left Africa it wasn't the impressive reports or grand plans from our staff meeting that stayed with me. It was the diverse array of people I'd met and the conversations I'd had. The English missionary family with whom I stayed in Livingstone who had eked out a meager existence for more than 30 years; the Sri Lankan engineer who described the invidious position of Asians in African society; the pool attendant at the Intercontinental Hotel in Lusaka who worked 16 years to earn US$25 a month; the Australian High Commissioner and his wife who invited my colleagues and me to dinner after Elaine had hitched a ride with them. But none of these came close to John Denby.

As I arrived in London after my 12-hour flight from Lusaka I glanced out the plane window to see snow covering the tarmac. Before landing the captain announced that the outside temperature was -5°C. When we left Zambia it was 25°C.

I thought of JD behind the wheel driving down the Great North Road and his farewell comment as he dropped me outside Lusaka. "I'll be thinking of you freezing your arse off in London." I went straight to the airport gift shop and bought a gray postcard that said 'London Fog'. I scribbled on it 'Thanks for the ride' and addressed it to 'King of the Road'.

YOU ARE NOT INDIAN,
ISN'T IT?

· · · · ·

It was a blistering summer day in eastern Maharashtra when the least thing seemed like a huge effort. I'd just endured another of my frequent battles with diarrhea, so I'd hardly eaten anything for more than 24 hours. I should have taken time out to recuperate, but knowing our staff were anticipating my arrival later that day I resolved to push on.

My destination was Rajapur, a small village close to the Madhya Pradesh border. It was the most easterly project in the state and the farthest to reach in my four-village circuit. My day began at 5:00 am when, after a quick cup of chai, I caught my first bus into Nagpur, from where I caught a second bus to the district town of Bhandara. Here I would take a third bus to the sub-district town of Tumsar, from where I would catch a final bus that, all things being equal — a phrase that could never have been invented in India — would get me to Rajapur by nightfall.

Travel days were a brief respite from village meetings, visits to government offices, sorting out project finances and mediating personal disputes. I felt a little like a British official in the days of the Raj going 'on tour' around his district and acting as magistrate, administrator and diplomat, but without a retinue of staff and servants to call on. Mine was a solitary undertaking, without all the frills and on a minimal budget. I treasured my time in transit and used it for reading and reflection and occasionally dozing off, although Maharashtra State Road Transport Corporation (MSRTC) buses and the roads on which they traveled were not built with this in mind. I tried not to engage with others; there was plenty of that once I reached a village or town.

At the Bhandara bus station I located my bus by following my usual rule of thumb — read the destination on the front of the bus, check with three people to see if at least two agreed, and then use my best judgment. My ability to read Devanagari script had improved markedly since I arrived in India two years before, but not by employing a tutor or studying grammar. The former I couldn't afford and the latter failed to sustain my interest. Instead, I used endless hours waiting in bus and train stations to read the plethora of advertisements that leer at you at every turn, many of them in both Marathi and English. The phonetic nature of Sanskrit languages made this seem more like a game than an intellectual exercise.

When the Tumsar bus pulled in I felt elated as I recognized its name right away. But finding the bus was one thing; getting on it and grabbing a seat entirely another. Despite their checkered history as a colonial power, the British did bequeath to India a number of things that have stood the test of time — a semblance of a democracy, a vast railway network that transports more than 30 million people a day, the great game of cricket, and not least, that noble institution, the queue. But like most things Indian, the queue had evolved its own distinctive qualities in the Subcontinent. Sometimes people abided by the first-come-first-served principle but it would take just one overly zealous type to jump the queue and it could quickly dissolve into a melee with much yelling and name calling.

Not feeling like taking on the masses that day, I prayed to Lord Ganesh — the remover of obstacles — to prevent such an occurrence. He must have been tuned in to my wavelength because everything seemed to be going smoothly. Since I was about half way down the queue, I knew I had a good chance of scoring a seat, so long as the ingenious Indian method of 'reserving' a seat by tossing a handkerchief through open windows didn't claim all seats in advance. I'd forgotten to bring my handkerchief that morning so I was at a distinct disadvantage.

But just as I reached the bottom step at the bus door another body mysteriously materialized and forced its way in front of me. My protestations in English were of no avail and my limited swearing vocabulary in Marathi didn't encompass the situation at hand. I was tempted to do what an American colleague — a former Presbyterian clergyman no less — told me was a failsafe method he had perfected in such situations. Carefully lift your foot and bring it down with a crunch on top of the offending one. While the person whose foot you had just mutilated was letting you know what a heinous crime you had committed, you would apologize profusely and quickly secure your place in the line. This time decorum got the better of me and I let the rogue go.

As soon as I was safely in the bus I lunged at the first available seat. It happened to be a window seat, the prize I was after. Sitting on the aisle side of a seat in a MSRTC bus often became a fine balancing act, as you struggled to remain seated while the bus hurtled around hairpin bends on gravel roads. Although the seats were built for two people, quite often three would cram into them. Even if you were lucky to score just one other passenger alongside you, the minimum-width seats didn't offer much room. And should your fellow occupant be someone who didn't subscribe to the one-person-per-half-seat rule, you'd be better off standing up. At least I thought so. Indians seemed to prefer a fraction of a seat to nothing at all and were masters at sitting on the merest sliver.

Moments after I had claimed my precious space someone plopped himself down beside me. A quick glance told me he was a slim, middle-aged man, most likely a civil servant, another of those treasured legacies of the British Raj. His faded white, short-sleeved shirt and tapered, dark gray trousers were almost a uniform for the ubiquitous Indian government clerk. They were probably exactly what civil servants wore in India a hundred years before. The dark blue fountain pen with fake gold trim in his shirt pocket radiated 'bureaucrat' like a flashing red light.

Fearing I might be in for one of those tell-me-all-about-you conversations, I took the offensive and opened the newspaper I had bought at the bus station kiosk and shrouded myself in it from ear to ear. Being a Marathi paper must have added to the curiosity of my fellow traveler. What he didn't know was that after having read the headlines I could understand little else, except the score of the current Australia-India cricket match, whose players' names I could read phonetically and whose batting and bowling figures were presented according to standard cricket protocol. This allowed me to get a feel for what had happened and where the game was heading.

As I immersed myself in this, I had a distinct feeling that my fellow passenger was about to burst on to center stage with his opening line. It was like being in a sauna, where the temperature rises and the steam increases until you can't stand it any longer. For 15 minutes he had held back, denying himself the one thing he probably wanted more than anything at that moment — to find out who was this fair-skinned, gaunt young man next to him and what on earth he was doing in this far-flung corner of Maharashtra in the middle of summer.

Finally he reached breaking point. A slender finger appeared around the edge of my newspaper and ever so gently peeled back the page to reveal a bespectacled face with two deep brown eyes staring straight at me. I felt I had been stripped naked. An alien had invaded my private space, private that is from my purely Western point of view. Few Indians know the luxury of privacy.

I took a deep breath and wondered what would be his next move. Then in the most polite textbook English he could muster my companion cleared his throat and let forth the question that was burning a hole in his being.

"Excuse me sir, but I think it is, that you are not Indian, isn't it?"

Of the six million Indians traveling on more than 14,000 buses that day in Maharashtra I had to sit beside this particular one. I resented his intrusion into my personal world, but rationalized it as Indian curiosity at encountering a foreigner. However, I couldn't help wondering if it was something more. In a society in which caste is so firmly embedded maybe even foreigners need to be placed in their niche. In the grand scheme of things there was a slot for everyone, from untouchables to the pantheon of gods. Certain humans, such as film stars, corporate magnates and cricket heroes, seemed to compete with the gods and at times were almost indistinguishable from them.

Having made his bold opening move, my companion lost no time in following it up. The questions came thick and fast, in fairly predictable order.

"What is your good name, may I ask?"

Not sure about the may, but he certainly had.

"What is your native place?"

Essential information, like rank and serial number.

"What brings you to India side?"

In India, everything has sides. Delhi side, Calcutta side, even India itself.

"You have visited Taj Mahal?"

Of course everyone comes to India to do this, don't they?

"Are you liking Indian food?"

Tossing out a few of my favorite dishes like palak paneer and chicken shahi korma always scored points on this one, although best to keep it vegetarian.

Are you married?

Dangerous not to answer in the affirmative even if you have no intention of getting married. Definitely don't mention you are gay.

"Your mummy and daddy, they are in Australia, yar?"

After explaining that my father had 'expired' — in India you don't die, you expire, like out-of-date coupons — the conversation took a different turn.

"So who is looking after your mummy?"

"She does pretty well on her own" is not an adequate answer. Beware of mentioning nursing homes and the like.

"You must be following cricket, isn't it?"

Of course I must, I'm male and I'm an Australian. Fortunately I did, and this was my chance to segue away from my personal information. Praising several of India's cricketing greats never hurt.

Half an hour later I was rescued from my KGB-like interrogation by our arrival at the Tumsar bus station. After helping me check when my next bus would depart, my companion was reluctant to let me go. Discovering me seemed the highlight of his day, if not week, month, year or more. He insisted we celebrate the occasion with a visit to the station refreshment room.

"What will you take? Hot or cold?" he asked, as if life could be reduced to this simple choice. Given the temperature that day I opted for the latter.

"You are liking Limca or Thums Up?"

While neither excited me, I preferred a gaseous, artificial lemon-flavored drink to India's answer to Coca-Cola.

"Do Limca," he barked at a barefoot young boy in a tattered grey T-shirt who condescended to wait on us.

When the bottles arrived they were neither hot nor cold but the usual lukewarm. Our conversation picked up where it had left off on the bus. This time it was my turn to ask the questions. The answers were brief and confirmed most of my hunches.

"And where do you live, sir?"

"Here only, in Tumsar."

"What kind of work do you do?"

"I'm assistant deputy sub-inspector with PWD."

"You have children?"

"One son and two daughters," he admitted, as if cursed with bad luck.

This question caused the conversation to take a sharp turn and allowed him to regain the initiative.

"You are coming back through Tumsar at the end of the week, is it? You must come and take food with us. You can stay overnight and leave next morning."

India's famous hospitality had reared its generous head once more. I had only met this stranger a few hours before and he was inviting me into the bosom of his family life. The old 'guest is a god' mantra kept playing in my head. His offer sounded more like a command and one I dare not refuse.

I glanced at my watch, then outside in the direction of the Rajapur bus.

"Just I am going now," he said. "I tell you what. You do one thing. When you come back to Tumsar, you phone me at my office," he said, thrusting a well-worn government card into my hand. "I will send my peon to meet you. He knows short cut to my house. No need for long cut."

I thanked my companion profusely for his kind invitation and promised I'd do my 'level best' to respond to it. It was time to head for my next bus and another queue.

WALLS AND FENCES

. . . . .

Christmas 1984 was my first in Europe and I was looking forward to it like a young child. My friend Russel and I traveled from Brussels to Frankfurt to celebrate with colleagues there. This year our NGO staff worldwide had decided to experiment with a 'pilgrimage'. Individuals, families or groups were to visit a place of special significance and share their reflections afterwards. Along with Wayne, an American, and Thekla, a German, Russel and I decided to make our pilgrimage to Dachau Concentration Camp near Munich. Having arrived in Belgium a few months before, I wanted to try to understand what it meant to be European forty years after the continent had endured the most shocking upheaval the world had known. Dachau seemed a good place to start.

December in Germany can be brutally cold yet astonishingly beautiful. The Christmas Market in Frankfurt's main square was the epitome of that. With colored lights and seasonal music, the festooned stalls around Römerberg plaza dazzled the eyes. The 30-meter illuminated tree that soared above the stalls and the undulating horses on the carousel created a surreal atmosphere and the scent of cinnamon mixed with hot mulled wine followed me wherever I went. I bought a box of Christmas cards depicting the market to try to convey to friends and family how enchanting this place was. Every craft was exquisitely carved, every food item perfectly presented. It all fitted together like a huge jigsaw puzzle to produce an unparalleled spectacle. Who were these people who could create such a stunning masterpiece?

As we prepared for the 385-kilometer drive to Munich we heard weather reports of dropping temperatures and possible snow storms. Although our little Volkswagen was showing its age we trusted it would get us there and back safely, since most of the journey was on an autobahn. We left early on Christmas Eve morning to give ourselves time to reach our destination and return the same day. Our route took us through some of Germany's premier wine country and past Nuremberg with its gruesome history of Nazi rallies and war crimes trials. When I stepped out of the car at Dachau I was overwhelmed by the sub-freezing temperature. Wearing a thick woolen coat, long underwear, a scarf and cap, I was still frozen to the bone. I couldn't conceive how scantily clad, emaciated prisoners survived this weather under appalling conditions.

After entering the main gate we headed for the museum, one of the few original buildings remaining. It was hard to conceive that floggings and hangings took place here. It now housed photographic exhibitions and a film that provided a useful but disturbing orientation to the camp. I learned many things, most of which I'd rather not have known. One that particularly struck with me was that Dachau was the prototype concentration camp established in March 1933, six years before the outbreak of war. It spawned numerous other camps across Europe and more than 150 satellites camps in its vicinity.

Between 1933 and the end of the war Dachau's role changed several times. It began as an internment center for Germans whose political or ideological views conflicted with those of the ruling National Socialists. Following the passage of the Nuremberg Laws institutionalizing racial discrimination it received large numbers of 'anti-social elements' — Jews, Jehovah Witnesses, Protestant and Catholic clergy, Sinti and Roma Gypsies, homosexuals and others. When the war started it became an instrument of extermination, especially for the intelligentsia from occupied territories.

Of all the exhibits one of the most chilling was a chart depicting the distinguishing insignias worn by prisoners. With classic German rationality, the SS had created a matrix of types of prisoners depicted by different colors and symbols. They seemed particularly fond of triangles. Homosexuals wore a pink triangle, Jews a yellow star — a combination of two triangles. Everyone was reduced to a category, part of the Nazi effort to dehumanize and eradicate those who stood in their way of creating a master race. It also let guards quickly identify prisoners for special treatment. Throughout its grim history more than 200,000 prisoners from 30 countries filed through Dachau's main gate, which bore the ominous and cynical words 'Arbeit Macht Frei' (Work makes you free). Nearly 32,000 died.

Another aspect of Dachau also left an indelible impression on me. From 1942 on, the camp was used for 'medical experiments'. Some were conducted for the German Air Force for high-altitude flying and reviving aircrew shot down over the sea. Subjects were immersed fully dressed in ice cold water for up 90 minutes or stripped naked and left to stand in the cold for hours. Equally barbaric was the attempt to find a cure for malaria that was killing German soldiers in North

Africa. Young Polish priests were popular candidates for this. Several hundred died from malaria and others succumbed to conditions brought on by it or due to overdoses. Just before he was hanged, the perpetrator of these grisly crimes justified them by saying they were done for the good of mankind.

After this unsettling introduction, Russel and I headed out into the freezing parade ground. I wondered how much more of this we could stomach. The farther we went, the less we said. Of the original barracks, only two remained. But these sanitized recreations didn't convey the horror of the real thing. They were divided into four dormitories, each designed to house 52 prisoners. Two dorms shared one washroom and lavatory. As the war progressed up to 1,600 prisoners lived in one dormitory. Many died of typhus caused by body lice.

As we walked through the empty camp grounds I struggled to imagine this place 40 years before. The putrid smells and the skeletal bodies escaped me. But one thing did not — the cold. We stepped up our pace as we headed to the end of the vast compound, gravel crunching beneath our feet. Our destination was the Protestant Church of Reconciliation which, along with Catholic and Jewish buildings, stood in stark contrast to former camp structures. The irregular shape of the rooms belied the sense of organized terror that pervaded the rest of the camp. After descending the semi-circular steps we passed through a dark, narrow entrance into a light-flooded courtyard. On a steel gate was an engraving from the 17th psalm: 'Hide me under the shadow of thy wings'.

While the architecture was an address, it set the stage for a much greater surprise. As we approached the door to the main meeting room we were taken aback by a large sign that read 'Ausstellung: Homosexualität und Politik seit 1900' (Exhibition on Homosexuality and Politics since 1900). I looked at Russel and gasped.

"I don't believe this! We've come all this way for our pilgrimage and we find an exhibition on gays in Germany."

The irony was not lost on Russel either. As two gay men we had been finding our way since we met in Chicago earlier that year. Coming out to the community in which we lived and worked had been a gradual and challenging process. Neither of us was out to our parents. But our struggles were nothing compared to those suffered by LGBT men and women in Germany under the Third Reich. It was as though we had been led to this place at this time. Our pilgrimage now took on a much more personal and poignant quality.

The exhibition was jointly sponsored by the Protestant Church of Reconciliation and a local gay Christian group. One of their members, an affable young man named Bernhard, became our guide and translator. He told us that about 10,000 homosexual prisoners were sent to concentration camps during Hitler's 12-year regime. In the camps they were not only singled out by their captors for unusually cruel treatment, they were also persecuted by fellow inmates, which contributed to their abnormally high death rate. In addition, they were given dangerous work and used as target practice by the SS. Camp doctors experimented on them to try to find a 'gay gene' to cure Aryan children who showed same-sex tendencies.

Bernhard's comments left me numb. Had I been born in a different time and place, I could have been part of this catastrophic human abasement. Before we left, Bernhard gave me brochures about the plight of gays in Germany today and contact information for organizations and resource groups. Meeting a young gay German who dared to tell what had happened in his country and who was committed to ensuring it was never repeated was a deep address.

Darkness was quickly falling, along with the temperature. Back in our car a brooding silence hung over the group. No one wanted to break it. We had a long drive back to Frankfurt and the weather looked threatening but we decided to head into Munich for a quick meal before hitting the road. We drove around block after block but all restaurants and cafes were closed. Thekla explained that Christmas Eve is when most German families celebrate Christmas dinner, usually at home. Eventually we spotted a place that appeared open so Thekla went to investigate. She returned to inform us that they were only taking people with reservations.

Although we were not hungry when we left Dachau, none of us wished to drive four or five hours back to Frankfurt on an empty stomach. Surely in a city the size of Munich something would be open, Christmas Eve or not. Just as we were about to give up, Russel yelled out.

"Look, over there. It's a Turkish restaurant. And I think it's open!"

The mood in the car lightened considerably. Although the restaurant was crowded, there were a couple of empty tables. After a delicious meal of kebabs and falafel, stuffed eggplant and tomato pilaf, we left an hour later, satiated and grateful for Germany's Turkish Muslim community.

By the time we hit the autobahn it was snowing heavily. Mercedes and BMWs zipped past like shooting stars. The driving snow limited visibility so we changed drivers frequently. Some of us dozed but I found myself reflecting on our afternoon. I also couldn't help think of the glamorous spectacle I'd witnessed at the Frankfurt Christmas Market a few days before. How was it possible that the same people who created such magical artistry could be responsible for such human degradation and suffering? The two seemed irreconcilable.

* * *

Most of my images of Berlin were formed from spy novels or war movies, as well as Western media depictions of West Germany as free and prosperous and East Germany as dull, restrictive and underdeveloped. While there may have been some truth in these generalizations, I wanted to see for myself. The opportunity to do so came unexpectedly in 1986 when I was working at our NGO's international secretariat in Brussels. The West German government invited our institute to help lead a training program for government employees from ten Asian countries. Our segment of the eight-week course was a three-day module entitled 'People's Participation: A Key to Project Success'. My colleague Sandy and I teamed up to do this.

We were still trying to sleep after the overnight train ride from Brussels when there was banging on the door. It was thrust open, the light went on, and an authoritative voice barked, "Guten Morgen, Pass bitte!" I looked at my watch. It was a little after 4:00 am. We were just recovering from this assault when another knock came. "Guten Morgen, Fahrkarten bitte." After this we resigned ourselves to an early start to the day. But we couldn't sit and enjoy the view for the next two hours because the railway line was enclosed in a fortified corridor. Not only was Berlin within East Germany but West Berlin was an island unto itself, surrounded by the famous wall.

On arrival in West Berlin we were met by Gerd who had contracted us to do the course. The dilapidated railway station presented a stark contrast to the clinically clean and colorful stations in the rest of West Germany. It was dirty, drab and undergoing repairs. As we made our way through the scaffolding to the car park, Gerd explained that the East German authorities had just granted West Berlin the right to operate the railway in the city. Until then little money had been spent on maintaining the station, so it had fallen into disrepair, like many stations in East Germany.

Driving through Berlin early on a Sunday morning was an eerie experience. If we had gone down the famous Kufürstendamm boulevard we would have seen people carrying on from the night before or having early morning coffee. Instead, we skirted the city center and made for the outer suburb where we would to be staying. The Brandenburg Gate stood like an abandoned fortress. It was hard to imagine it was once one of the busiest intersections in Europe. Access was blocked on one side by the Wall and the other was patrolled by armed guards. East German and Russian flags flew above the gate, while nearby on top of a building was the West German flag — reminders of the divided city Berlin had been since 13th August 1961.

When we arrived at our lodgings Sandy and I did a second take. Set in lush grounds on the shores of the picturesque lake Tegelsee was a grand mansion. Built in 1908 as the home of the prominent German industrialist Ernst Borsig, it exuded power and wealth, from the massive bathroom in the guest suite to the security post at the front gate. During the Second World War the villa had become the Third Reich's Finance Academy. I conjured up images of SS troops patrolling the grounds or conferring in the grand salons. Nowadays, Villa Borsig was being put to more laudable use by the German Foundation for International Development as a conference and training center.

In this delightful location we set about demonstrating how to elicit people's participation in development. We were coming in at the beginning of the seventh week of the program, so all 25 participants and the two German coordinators were fairly burned out. Most participants had had enough of Europe and were thinking only about going home to family, warmer climates and hot, spicy food. They'd also had their fill of outside consultants pouring wisdom down their throats.

The first day was tough but we made it through thanks to Sandy's effervescent style and expert facilitation skills. However, we needed something to get the second day off to a flying start. Over breakfast we managed to persuade the Filipino contingent to give a rendition of one of their well-known love songs, the tune for which was familiar to us from our village work in the Philippines. Singing was not as alien to the Asians as it was to the Germans and proved to be a great ice-breaker. As the course progressed we convinced our German colleagues of its virtues. One decided to teach participants an old German song about the evils of coffee drinking. It was a big hit that gave everyone permission to follow suit. The mood changed dramatically.

The day after the course ended Sandy and I were invited to join the group in an excursion and dinner. We toured well-known sites, the most dramatic of which was the famous Glienicke Bridge — 'the bridge of spies' — linking East and West Berlin. During the Cold War it was used for prisoner exchanges, the most recent being earlier that year when the Jewish human rights activist Anatoly Shcharansky and three Western agents were swapped for five Eastern Bloc agents. As we looked across the lake to the other side we saw the same kind of houses as those on the western side, except these were empty or used by the border police. All land 500 meters back from the shore was off limits and equipped with anti-escape devices. In the middle of the lake were marker buoys indicating the boundary between the two Berlins, which birds perched on as if in disdain of this human folly.

From the bridge we drove to a restaurant where the West Berlin Senate was hosting our delegation to a farewell dinner. Built as an old hunting lodge, the restaurant was situated in a forest where the kings of Prussia used to hunt wild boars. Fortunately, the only boars we saw were securely caged. Upon arrival I was invited to sit at the head table next to our host from the Berlin Senate, Herr Lohr. I was nervous being assigned such a position and had to draw on everything I'd learned in India about being the feted guest. After listening to several welcome speeches and votes of thanks, we began our meal — a hearty, four-course affair that began with creamy potato soup and ended with generous portions of apple strudel and cream.

We weren't far into the meal when Herr Lohr rose and tapped on his glass with a spoon. His address was not the most enlightened presentation on development but he delivered it with great passion, no doubt enhanced by the generous quantities of Mosel wine that had been flowing freely. When he resumed his seat conversation between us picked up pace. I remember espousing the virtues of Australian wine, while pointing out that it was largely German settlers we had to thank for that. Somehow this segued into how Australians make bush tea in a 'billy can' and flavor it with eucalyptus leaves. This fascinated Herr Lohr, who couldn't wait to visit the Land Down Under. When we parted company for the evening he beamed with pride as he gripped my hand and gave it a prolonged shake. I felt I'd done my bit for Australian-German relations.

But the night was not quite over. Sandy, who had won everyone's heart, was leaving on the night train to Brussels, while I stayed on a few days. As she departed for the station, the entire bus of Asians, Latin Americans and Germans burst into song with a rousing rendition of a ditty she had taught them. Strains of 'Free, free, free to decide' to the tune of 'Hey Ho, Nobody Home' wafted through the bus windows. It was a touching sight but not without irony. Within a few kilometers millions of East Germans were yet to experience the reality these words were celebrating.

Following Sandy's departure I had two days to explore Berlin. My starting point was the working-class area of West Berlin known as Kreuzberg, home to many Turkish guest workers. Our NGO had had one of its Human Development Projects in Kreuzberg, so I was keen to visit the neighborhood. Unfortunately, my one contact was out of town, so I browsed on my own. Banners denouncing nuclear power in the aftermath of the recent Chernobyl disaster hung from balconies. I tracked down the Cafe zur Laterne that had been used during the project for community gatherings and ordered a large Berliner Pils and a doner kebab.

From Kreuzberg I followed the Wall several kilometers to the famous crossing point, Checkpoint Charlie. The Wall was covered with graffiti, ranging from brightly colored Picasso-like creations to Statues of Liberty. Messages were equally varied from 'Smash the Wall' to 'There won't be a Wall in Heaven' and 'Happy 25th Birthday'. At regular intervals from raised platforms I could see across to the other side and the no man's land between, replete with anti-escape devices, including automatic-firing weapons. Seventy-five people had died trying to cross the Wall, most shot by East German border guards.

But not all guards performed their duty so well. When I entered the Haus am Checkpoint Charlie museum — a converted apartment house next to the crossover point — the first thing I noticed was a poster honoring those East German border guards who deliberately misfired at fleeing targets. Exhibits bore testimony to the courage and ingenuity of those who sought to flee the East — a rust-colored Opel sedan with armor plating and concrete-filled doors, a wooden wagon that removed dirt from a tunnel through which 57 refugees escaped, and an improvised chair lift in which a family of three escaped. The week after I left a family crashed through the checkpoint barriers in a truck.

The next day would be my last and I was determined to visit East Berlin, my first foray behind the Iron Curtain. I'd been told the border crossing could take an hour or more, along with the mandatory exchange of a minimum 25 West German D-Marks for East German Ostmarks, so I was pleasantly surprised when I was through in 15 minutes. Since the creation of the border by East Berlin was in contravention of the agreement governing Berlin it was not a legal border, but with thousands of tourists crossing daily into East Berlin it provided a welcome source of foreign exchange for East Germany.

As soon as I left Friedrichstrasse station I made for Unten den Linden. Regaled as 'the Champs Élysées of the North', this sprawling boulevard that once bustled with pedestrians now only attracted a sprinkling of tourists. I had never experienced such expansiveness in a city. The buildings were majestic, many having been rebuilt since the war and some like the Volkskammer (People's Chamber) were new. Except for the occasional East German Trabbi or Russian Lada puttering along, traffic barely existed. As I walked I chanced upon the Changing of the Guard at the New Guard House. Goose-stepping young soldiers guarding this shrine in remembrance to victims of fascism and militarism had an ironic twist.

Nearby was the Museum of German History, so I thought I'd see how the East Germans told their side of the story. Unsure where to begin, I decided to take a rational Germanic approach, starting with prehistory, progressing to the Roman era, and on through the Middle Ages. The quality of the exhibits was impressive — dioramas of battles with miniature figures, scale models of entire medieval cities, blood-thirsty weapons leering at me from all directions. They led me to reflect on the number of times people have built walls to shut out barbarians, maintain their privacy and privileges, or just keep 'the other' at arms' length. Berlin was unusual in that it had built a wall through a city.

After two and a half hours my stomach was sending out Mayday signals, so I started looking for restaurants. I couldn't spot any wurst vendors or doner kebab stands and being Saturday shops had closed at 1:00 pm. So I decided to head to the Chamber of the People. Surely such a place took care of the people's stomachs as well as their hearts and minds. I found several restaurants there but each had long lines trailing out their doors. I joined one but after half an hour glued to the same spot I gave up on that queue and tried another, with the same result. In desperation, I exited the Chamber of the People and crossed the monstrous Alexanderplatz.

Just as I was about to give up I spotted a sign pointing upstairs to a Czech restaurant. When I reached the door I was delighted to find only half a dozen people in front me. Behind me were four people from the People's Republic of China. I wanted to ask them if it was as difficult to find eating places in their people's republic as it was in this one but my Mandarin wasn't up to it. When the maître d' beckoned the next in line my heart started racing, until he made it clear that the Chinese would go first because they were a party of four and I a mere one.

Finally around 3:00 pm I sat down to lunch. It was not the haute cuisine we had indulged in two days before at the expense of the West German Senate, but I was so hungry anything passable seemed gastronomic. As I gazed out the window trying to make sense of this strange society, the waiter nearly absconded with my half-finished plate. He seemed much keener to get me out of there than to allow me in.

After lunch I decided to leave the main thoroughfares and hit the back streets. Old tenements that had escaped bombing during the war seemed fully occupied but in desperate need of repair. Both Berlins had undertaken massive housing construction since the war but with distinct differences. The repetitiveness in design of buildings here stood in stark contrast to the variety in West Berlin. But what I noticed most was the lack of color. Few buildings had been painted and there were no billboards clamoring for your attention. Some had murals on their walls but nothing like the dramatic scenes I witnessed in West Berlin. As much as I detest garish advertising and some avant-garde public art, its absence here was strangely disconcerting.

I had a few hours before heading back to West Berlin and still had Ostmarks to spend. I needed toothpaste but my chances of finding anything open were slim. Just when I thought this was futile I noticed a small shop with credit card signs in its window. I peered inside and saw an array of foreign goods, ranging from Swiss chocolates to Japanese VCRs. Noticing Colgate toothpaste labeled 2.50 I put my hand into my pocket and withdrew two Ostmarks and fifty pfennigs. The shop assistant looked at me in bewilderment as I offered her my East German marks. "Nein, nein" she said. "Amerikanische Dollar, mein Herr!" I had just encountered one of East Germany's foreign currency stores for those few who could afford them. Toothpaste could wait until I returned to West Berlin.

Given my minimal stipend, frugal nature and general dislike of shopping it was ironic to find myself having to spend money and couldn't. (It was illegal to take Ostmarks out of the country but why you'd want to I couldn't imagine.) Late in the afternoon I came across a cafe, so ordered coffee and picked up *The Berlin News*, the semi-official government paper. I turned to the sport page, brimming with information about the world swimming championships in Madrid, which East German women were dominating. We've since learned how their athletes achieved such feats, but then could only marvel at them.

As I meandered through the back streets of East Berlin, people were hanging out of windows gossiping, fixing their cars, drinking with friends in a pub. But there was none of the hubbub and the commercialism rampant just across the other side of the Wall. When I reflected on my day I was reminded of the need to always put one's immediate experiences into a larger context. As I crossed back over to West Berlin I found myself dwelling on the words of Richard von Weizsacker, former mayor of West Berlin and later president of the Federal Republic of Germany. In commemorating Berlin's 750th anniversary as a city he said:

> That the wall remains after 25 years is probably the most important proof of the fact that our feelings of belonging together, in East and West Germany, are as strong today as in the past. History has always provided fresh answers regarding the political structures of Central Europe. No political framework used by the Germans has ever lasted more than 100 years. It would thus run counter to our historical experience to believe that the situation that has existed since the erection of the Wall is history's final answer. The human desire for self-determination and freedom will, one way or another, continue to grow and assert itself. Berlin symbolizes that feeling for all of Eastern Europe.

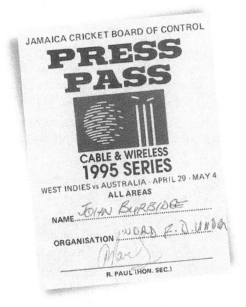

JAMAICA FAREWELL

or

My Short-lived Career as a Foreign Correspondent

· · · · ·

If it hadn't been for a cricket match I never would have taken this trip. But it wasn't just any cricket match. It was the final match in a four-game series in which the West Indies and Australia were one game all. It was 1995 and for 22 years no team had beaten the 'Windies' on their home turf and for 15 of those years no other team had beaten them at all. They were undisputed champions in international cricket but I had a hunch this Aussie team might just change that.

Since I was living in Seattle at the time Jamaica seemed the nearest place I could see a live international cricket match.

I'd been asked to go to Guatemala on a work assignment so decided to add a leg to Jamaica. But time was short and my finances were tight. When I checked my frequent-flyer program I discovered I had just enough miles to get me from Seattle to Miami and back, so I called the airline to see if there was a seat five days ahead. To my delight there was. Surprisingly, there were also plenty of seats on the Miami-Kingston leg. I was not expecting this, so I took it as a positive sign and focused on the next issue — where to stay in Kingston.

Every bed in Kingston and nearby towns would have been booked long ago or snapped up after the West Indies had squared the series. What to do? Then I remembered the village development project our NGO had had in Woburn Lawn in Jamaica's Blue Mountains. One of the project's expat staff now worked for the United Nations in New York, so I decided to give him a call to see if he could help.

"Well, there is someone," said Rob thoughtfully. "Right here in New York. Donrad Duncan was a tailor in the village. He married a young American volunteer, Kristin, and they live in Manhattan. I've got their number somewhere. Let me dig it out and I'll call you back."

Rob phoned me later that day with the couple's number. He also alerted them that they might be receiving a call from me, so when I phoned that evening I was warmly greeted by a pleasant Midwestern female voice.

"Strange you should call this week, John. Donrad's father died last week so he went down for the funeral. He's probably in Kingston right now at our apartment. I'll check with him to see what he can arrange and call you back. I'm sure it won't be a problem."

I had a growing sense I was meant to do this trip but I still had several hurdles to clear. A major one was how to get into the cricket ground, since tickets to the modest-sized stadium at Kingston's Sabina Park would have sold long ago and the cost of a black market ticket would have been out of reach. I needed help.

I turned to Neil Brandom, an Aussie who lived in Southern California and edited a monthly expat magazine, *Word From Down Under*. I had contributed a number of articles and enjoyed working with Neil.

"Gedday John. Good to hear from you mate. What's up?"

"Well, Neil, I know how much you love cricket and would like to publish something on the series between Australia and the West Indies, especially since our lads might just pull it off this time. I have to head down that way for work so I thought I'd do a little detour and try to see the final game. It's a long shot at such short notice but I might be able to do it. The main problem is, how do I get into the ground at this late stage?"

"No worries, mate," Neil assured me. "I'll write you a letter of introduction that says you work for this esteemed publication and request all authorities to render you any assistance you may need to fulfill your duties as a reporter. Howzat? Should do the trick. But given the short time, I'd better fax it to you rather than trust the mail."

Later that day my fax machine chugged to life and spewed out a barely legible piece of paper with *Word From Down Under* spread-eagled across the top in the latest MS-Word clip art style. Neil had many gifts but design and layout were not among them. However, he did have a genuine, if somewhat dated, sense of humor. Around the perimeter of the letterhead was a selection of classic Australian colloquialisms that included 'Don't come the raw prawn with me, sport', 'It's a bonzer time to boil the billy, but bugger me the blowies are bad' and 'As cold as a mother-in-law's breath'. Fortunately these pearls of wisdom were printed in such a small type they were barely readable.

But it was not these gems that caught my eye. It was the short paragraph in bold type that said 'We would appreciate your efforts to provide Mr. Burbidge with a press pass. Please also include Mr. Burbidge on the press list for any other relevant events.' I would have preferred these words to have been typed on fresh, white paper instead of a yellowy, coated fax but that wasn't to be. I slipped the page into an envelope and added it to my pile of things to pack.

Two days passed and I hadn't heard from Kristin. Knowing her husband was dealing with his father's death, I didn't expect my visit would be a high priority for him. But when I still hadn't heard the night before my departure, I called her. Donrad had been difficult to reach but she assured me my coming wouldn't be a problem and suggested I call from Miami the following morning. I headed to the airport bound for a country I'd never been to, not knowing where I'd stay once I arrived or if I'd get to see the game that was my reason for going.

Miami airport was like a zoo with all the cage doors open. I expected it to be busy but wasn't anticipating the chaos I encountered. I walked right to the end of a concourse to find a phone away from the hubbub and dialed Kristin.

"Good timing, John," she said. "I just spoke to Donrad. He said it'll be fine for you to stay in the apartment. He will be there when you arrive but he's flying back to the US the next day. Stay as long as you like. The housekeeper will look after you. He's trying to arrange for Royal Mowatt to meet you at the airport. He's a former project staffer who runs a taxi service. Just wait outside the main terminal. He'll collect you and take you to the apartment."

My anxiety level decreased. It was as though I only had to make the initial decision to do this trip and the rest would fall into place.

* * *

As our American Airlines 737 touched down at Kingston's airport a sense of nervous anticipation gripped my stomach. When I sidled up to the immigration booth and presented my passport I noticed how dejected the officer behind the counter looked. He saw my Australian passport and didn't ask the purpose of my visit.

"Lara just got out for 65," he said as he thumped a fresh page with a visitor's visa. Sixty-five runs was not a bad score for the average batsman, but coming from this West Indian superstar, who had blazed the record books with ethereal scores of 400 and 500 runs in an innings, this was trifling.

I retrieved my luggage and headed to the currency exchange, where the teller, like everyone else in the airport, was glued to his radio. "150 for 3," he reported as he handed me my Jamaican dollars. An American could be forgiven for thinking he was referring to the exchange rate, but this score update was much more valuable. It was early on the opening day of what could be a five-day game and Australia's bowlers had already dealt their opponents a serious blow.

I wandered out of the terminal and headed toward the taxi rank. Several drivers approached me but I assured them I had my own driver. Arriving passengers ebbed to a trickle so I dragged my case to a bit of shade and sat down on it. I took out my shortwave radio and had little trouble finding the game. As I waited, wickets tumbled. By the time Royal Mowatt arrived an hour and a half later several more West Indian batsmen were out. At the end of the afternoon Australia had dismissed the entire team for a meager 265 runs. I was delighted but disappointed I had missed the spectacle.

When Royal brought his 1975 Datsun to a halt at the compound gates I was sure he had the wrong address. Staring down at me was a 12-storey apartment building set in well-maintained grounds with white-painted rocks along the driveway. When I offered to pay Royal for his services he adamantly refused, insisting I was his guest and demanding that I contact him should I need to any time. He then escorted me into the building and whisked me into the elevator up to the sixth floor.

When the door opened I was greeted by a smart-looking young man who introduced himself as Donrad Duncan. His well-appointed clothes suggested more a New Yorker than a Blue Mountains villager and when he spoke his accent sounded somewhere between. He introduced me to his cousin and a young woman who was their cook-cum-housekeeper. Her food was delicious but her lilting Jamaican patois was almost incomprehensible.

I offered Donrad my condolences over his father's death and he asked me about my plans for the week. He and his cousin would be returning to New York the following afternoon but he'd be glad to help me in the morning. I explained my mission and the challenge of gaining entry to the ground. I delved into my bag and pulled out Neil's fax.

"My editor thought this should help me get me into the game," I said blithely.

Donrad screwed up his eyes as he looked it over but said he'd do what he could.

When we pulled up outside the main entrance to the ground my heart sank. The towering steel gates were closed, with hordes of fans surging in front of them. Police with Alsatian dogs wandered up and down trying to keep scores of ticketless young men from scaling the cyclone-mesh fence.

"Come on," said Donrad. "Where's that fax you showed me?"

I couldn't believe he was going to take on the crowd in front of the gate but I wasn't about to argue. I grabbed my bag and followed him like a shadow as he buffeted his way through the sea of bodies to the padlocked gates. He banged on the metal with his fist so hard I thought he'd damage his hand. A wrinkly face appeared in the small opening between the walls of steel. Donrad grabbed the fax and stuffed it in front of the gateman.

"I have an Australian reporter with me. He needs to get into the ground. Please let him in."

The middle-aged man perused the piece of paper with quizzical eyes. He knew press protocols and this wasn't one of them. Besides, media representatives would have presented their credentials on the first day of play, not the second.

"No," he said, handing the fax back to Donrad, ignoring his pleas and closing the gates.

No. That's all? No what? How dare he dismiss me like that! If only he knew how far I'd come and what it had taken to get here. I felt more sorry for Donrad than myself, but this initial rejection only steeled his resolve to try again.

"Let's go," he said. "There are other gates."

We set off at a torrid pace but when we arrived at the next gate we were greeted by the same mayhem as at the first. Again the gatekeeper responded negatively. I looked at Donrad and he sensed my dejection.

"This way mon," he yelled.

I followed him like an obedient dog. We trudged around most of the ground until we came to a third gate. Donrad rushed up to it and delivered his well-rehearsed speech. The young man on the other side took his time reviewing the fax. I held my breath and prayed to the cricket god which, given India's love of the game, I was sure existed somewhere in the Hindu pantheon.

Then as if my prayer was answered the gatekeeper slid open one of the doors just wide enough for me to edge through. I glanced at Donrad, shook his hand furiously, and said a heartfelt goodbye. I wouldn't see him again and could never repay him. I was astounded by the lengths to which he'd gone to help me. Before I left Jamaica a week later I would discover that such generosity was not unusual.

Once inside the ground I asked the gateman to direct me to the secretary's office. He pointed high up at the back of the members' stand. I thanked him and made a beeline for it. After knocking on the door I was ushered into the office of a mild-mannered gentleman who introduced himself as Ron Paul. I explained my situation and offered him the fax, which by now contained a number of finger marks.

"*Word From Down Under*, eh? Can't say I've heard of it. You're in the US, you say. What kind of readership do you have?"

I repeated everything I'd told him but enhanced our readership numbers considerably. I could hear his brain ticking over as he decided my fate. Then he went to the other side of his desk and opened a drawer. He pulled out a small light blue card and asked me to write my name on it. Under 'Organization' he penned Word F. D. Under and signed his name. I had gained admission to the ground for the duration of the game and at no cost. The words I liked best were 'All Areas' written just above my name. I headed straight for the press gallery at the opposite end of the ground.

* * *

By the time I reached the press box play had begun and the media reps were preparing their first dispatches to London, Sydney and throughout the Caribbean. Hunched over laptops they beavered away with headphones and binoculars as they followed the players' every move. Trying to appear as inconspicuous as possible, I sat near the back and opened my bag, careful not to expose my shortwave radio. I plugged in my earphones and scribbled a few words on my notepad.

As much as I wanted to follow the game, I kept being distracted by spectators nearby. If you've been brainwashed by movies that portray cricket as some genteel pursuit indulged by effete Englishmen who speak with plums in their mouths — 'Good shot, old boy' — forget it. Nothing could be further from the truth and here was living proof. The standing area known as The Mound attracted the more theatrically inclined Aussies and West Indians. During every break in play, as a DJ blasted the crowd with soca and reggae music, they joined in with didgeridoos, conch shells and horns.

But once play resumed silence reigned, as everyone waited to see what the Aussies could do with the bat. But when they lost their first three batsmen for a mere 73 runs it looked like the Windies had the upper hand. Enter the Waugh twins, Steve and Mark, two 30s-something lads from New South Wales. The West Indian bowlers seemed to wilt as the brothers began stroking the ball to all corners of the ground. When Mark was finally out for 126 they had amassed 231 runs. They had anchored the Australian innings and that most potent but elusive of forces in cricket — the psychological advantage — had swung in Australia's favor.

At the start of the third day's play Australia's first innings was looking good at 321 runs for 4 batsmen out. The home crowd was muted. Not even Bob Marley's beloved 'Don't worry... every little thing's going to be all right' blaring out over the PA system at regular intervals could rouse local supporters.

Steve Waugh batted on throughout the morning with masterful stroke play. When he glanced the ball to the boundary to bring up his 200, it was the Aussies' turn to let loose. Australian flags appeared from all corners of the ground as passionate supporters mobbed Steve Waugh in a frenzy of unabashed hero worship. A highly tolerant Jamaican police force didn't begrudge them their moment of glory.

When the Australian innings closed shortly after, Steve Waugh had been batting for nearly nine of its eleven hours. Australia's total of 531 runs was its second highest against the West Indies at Sabina Park. When the West Indians began the formidable task of scoring enough runs in their second innings to force the Australians to bat again, they were not up to the task. After their top three batsmen were dismissed by the close of play, local fans and commentators had all but conceded defeat.

That evening a reception was held for the players and media representatives at a five-star hotel. My press pass entitled me to attend, and as much as I relished the opportunity I was intimidated at the prospect of actually talking to the players. When I entered the reception room the Australians were huddled in one corner gripping cans of Fosters beer, while the West Indians mingled more among the crowd. Whether the Australians were instructed not to fraternize with the enemy or whether they lacked the capacity to do so I couldn't tell. But given that they held the upper hand in the game I would have thought they might have been a little more sociable.

After some careful maneuvering, I managed to corner one of Australia's leading batsmen and asked him how he found the game so far. He deflected my question and turned the conversation around to something that caught me by surprise.

"A lot of these guys are racist," he said, pointing in the direction of the West Indian team.

"Really? What do you mean by that?" I asked.

Before he could answer a West Indian official standing nearby made an innocent remark about the game that we couldn't help overhear.

"See what I mean?" said the Australian.

I couldn't detect anything remotely racist about what was said so it left me wondering about the Australian's perception and judgment. If his attitude was shared by the rest of the team it was cause for concern. As much as I admired their ability on the field it seemed that the Australians had considerable work to do as their country's cultural ambassadors. I later discovered I was not alone in harboring this concern.

Next day was a rest day, which proved fortuitous when drought-stricken Kingston was deluged by rain. I escaped the drenching when a former colleague offered to drive me over the mountains to a banana plantation managed by another ex-staff member. As we negotiated bone-rattling roads I immersed myself in the raw beauty of the lush tropical landscape. While the rain cleared the air in Kingston, the journey cleared my mind and returned me refreshed for the fourth day of the match.

Next morning every Jamaican seemed to have accepted the inevitable. Post-mortems droned on across the airwaves. But when Australia's ever-reliable wicketkeeper dropped a catch off the second ball of the day, the Windies had a brief reprieve. Two of their batsmen offered spirited resistance but Australia's master spin bowler — the 'Earl of Twirl' — struck back and the West Indies succumbed for a paltry 213 runs. Australia had won by an entire innings and 53 runs.

The Aussie fans took to the field en masse. Steve Waugh, who deservedly won both 'Man of the Match' and 'Man of the Series' awards, drove his newly acquired car around the ground with hordes of Jamaican school children in hot pursuit. So much for white linens, tea and scones, and modulated applause.

Buoyed by Australia's historic victory, I left the press box in an upbeat mood and joined the crowd pouring out of the ground. Taxis were scarce so I decided to take a bus back to the apartment. My hosts had warned me not to wander downtown since muggings and theft were common, but amid the throngs of spectators I felt at ease. However, the farther from the stadium I went, the thinner the crowds became. After about 15 minutes I found myself alone in a back street so stepped up my pace, frequently glancing over my shoulder to make sure I wasn't being followed.

I had just turned a corner when a group of young men approached from the opposite direction. I pretended not to notice them and continued at a fair clip. As soon as I'd passed them I looked back and saw they were now heading in my direction. Holding my bag close to my chest, I took off like a sprinter out of the blocks. One of them yelled at me but I kept running until I reached an alleyway and entered a crowded market. I rushed into first store I came to and tried to explain my predicament to the bewildered shopkeeper.

"So many tourists here for the cricket. Easy prey for those young scoundrels. You've got to be very careful mon," he said.

"Yes, I know. I've been warned. Can you tell me how I get to the bus depot from here?"

"Just down this road two blocks and around the corner. I'll take you there."

I thanked him for his kind offer and protested that it wasn't necessary, but he insisted.

"Mary," he yelled into the back of the store. "Watch the shop for me. I'm going out for a few minutes."

When we reached the bus station he asked my destination and made sure I was on the correct bus before he left. I was the only non-Jamaican on board; most passengers appeared to be returning home after work or shopping in the market. As I sat I found myself reflecting on the day. How quickly the euphoria of the game had been replaced by fear. Why do such highs and lows often occur so closely together? I wondered. How fortunate I'd been to find the shopkeeper when I needed him. Indeed, my entire trip had ridden on the backs of so many kind and caring souls.

* * *

Once ensconced in the apartment I considered my options for the next few days before flying back to Miami. My main task was to write up the story of the game and send it to Neil. I needed a computer or even typewriter but since Donrad had left I had to look elsewhere for help. Another former colleague had indicated he was keen to meet me so I gave him a call. Norris was a tall, lanky guy with a mellow voice and slow speech. Over dinner we chatted about our lives and work. I told him I had to write up my story and he assured me it wouldn't be a problem. I had sketched an outline of the article in my head but my deadline was fast approaching so I needed to write.

Over the next two days Norris and I spent a lot of time together. I enjoyed his company and he arranged meetings with people for other articles I was working on. But I kept wondering when I would have access to a computer or typewriter. When nothing had appeared the day before my departure I began to panic. I wrote a rough draft by hand and phoned Neil to apprise him of the situation.

"Hey Neil, it's your man in Kingston. Great game. I've got a good story but I'm having a hell of a time finding somewhere to type it up. I may have to write it in longhand and fax it to you."

"Not a problem. I can handle that. I've reserved you a page but I'll need your copy by the day after tomorrow."

As soon as I put the phone down I took out my notes and began transcribing them in large, capital letters. I left clear white spaces between paragraphs, included recommendations on photographs and titles, and added layout instructions, before signing it with Neil's favorite salutation, 'Chough'.

I urgently had to find a fax machine and again Norris assured me it was no problem. But when I left for the airport the following day I still hadn't located one. If there was one at the airport, I never found it. I had no choice but to wait until I arrived back in the US.

As soon as I reached Miami I headed to the American Airlines Admirals Club lounge and related my tale of woe to the receptionist. As an economy-class passenger I wasn't entitled to use these facilities but I have known airlines to bend the rules at times. Alas, this was not one of them. I trudged the length and breadth of Miami airport until finally I found a fax machine. I dispatched my story and prayed that Neil would receive it in time.

A couple of weeks later after I'd returned to Seattle my copy of *Word From Down Under* appeared in the mail. I opened it and held my breath as I read my article. It was word for word as I'd written it. Neil had squeezed in two photos from the game and even did the opening paragraph in italics. I was jubilant. He'd added: "We've taken a page of a tight newsletter for this cricket piece. However, this is nothing compared to the coverage allocated in Australia where, with no America's Cup glory to report, the cricket win was plastered all over the front page of most newspapers." I filed this in my back-handed compliments folder.

I was pleased to have contributed my little bit to this headline story, even if in such a nondescript publication as *WFDU*. I doubt other reporters covering the game faced the challenges I did but I bet none of them met such incredible people as I had either. A few weeks later I received a letter from Neil, with a check and slip of paper on which he'd scrawled 'Thanks, cobber!' He also included an e-mail he'd received from a subscriber. It read:

> Just wanted to say a quick word about the article on the
> fourth cricket test by John Burbidge. It was a brilliant

piece evoking those same emotions I felt when reading the *Sydney Morning Herald* articles my brother sent me. And good on you for making it a full page. This is easily the biggest Australian sporting success story for many years and it deserved full coverage. Pass on my congratulations to John Burbidge on a great article. It made me proud to be an Australian too.

DERAILED

· · · · ·

Trains have figured prominently in my life, for better and for worse. I have traveled on them across Australia and India, North America and Europe. In some I have luxuriated in cozy compartments with pull-down beds and early morning 'bed tea'; in others I have stood for hours in grossly overcrowded carriages with hundreds of others. I have made some of my most memorable contacts on trains and I nearly suffered a serious accident by jumping from one departing a station. Crossing Australia by train as a young boy I was introduced to fine dining, multiple meal choices and printed menus with phrases like 'compote de fruits'. I was held spellbound as a red-headed waiter waltzed down the aisle with outstretched arms laden with dinner plates.

My first train journey occurred when I was nine, from my home city of Perth to York, a bucolic town 100 kilometers east. While the distance was short it seemed an enormous undertaking at the time. It was Easter long weekend and my family was visiting the farm of friends near York. They sent me ahead so I could experience farm life and spend time with our friends' home-schooled daughter who rarely had other playmates. Little did they know that this modest venture was preparing me for much greater rail exploits in later life, two of which are especially memorable.

* * *

1963 wasn't a particularly auspicious year but I had just completed first-year high school and was enjoying summer holidays. I was also entering my growth spurt. My grandmother commented how my voice had changed and I noticed hair appearing in parts of my body where it hadn't been before. I was a member of Fremantle YMCA, which had challenged me physically with programs like gymnastics and fencing, as well as emotionally as I tried to deal with my propensity to stutter in stressful situations. I recoiled when called upon to thank guest speakers or lead the club ritual. When the opportunity came to participate in a national 'youth parliament' in Brisbane, I had mixed feelings. I couldn't imagine debating or making a speech but I was excited at the prospect of seeing more of Australia than the southwest corner in which I grew up. My parents had sent me to YMCA camps so this seemed like a logical next step, albeit longer and more expensive. Perhaps they saw it as a way to expand my horizons and increase my self-confidence, although we never talked about such things.

Getting to Brisbane and back was as much a challenge as the youth parliament itself. In those days traveling across the country by train was a complicated affair. Due to quirks of colonial history Australia had three rail gauges — 3 feet 6 inches (107 cm), 4 feet 8.5 inches (144 cm), and 5 feet 3 inches (160 cm) — depending which state you were in and even within the same state. To travel from Perth to Brisbane passengers had to change trains five times. This usually involved getting off a train on one side of the platform and hauling your luggage to an awaiting train on the other.

We broke our week-long, trans-continental journey for a few hours in Adelaide, where I was met by relatives, and in Melbourne and Sydney, where we stayed in YMCA hostels, the likes of which I'd never seen. Their primary attraction was the indoor swimming pools where we spent a good deal of our time. When we finally made it to Brisbane I was unprepared for its sapping humidity and nightly hordes of mosquitoes. I recall little of the conference itself, but I do remember declining an invitation to lead grace one morning. The thought of embarrassing myself in front of the entire gathering was more than I could bear.

After two weeks it was time to return home by doing the 5,600-kilometer journey in reverse. All went smoothly until we left Port Augusta in South Australia for the long haul west. The railway line between South Australia and Western Australia crosses the Nullarbor (no tree) Plain, a vast, semi-arid limestone desert where plants and animals are few and people even fewer. It includes the longest straight stretch of rail line in the world — 478 kilometers. It was in this section, near the small siding of Naretha, where our great rail journey took a turn for the worse. Even among the thread of tiny settlements that serviced the Trans-Australian Railway, Naretha barely scored a mention. A drop-off point for mail and supplies to nearby stations, it had a rock crushing plant for railway ballast and a bakery that provided fresh bread for trains and workers. But around 3:00 pm on Saturday 19th January 1963 Naretha made it into the history books.

It was summer and temperatures were well over the century Fahrenheit. The maximum that day at nearby Rawlinna was

41.7 °C in the shade. Our train consisted of 16 carriages and was pulled by two 1,800-horsepower diesel locomotives. Extra carriages had been added for the large number of Western Australians returning home from holidays in the east. Some of us were sleeping, others playing cards or reading. The train slowed to about 65 kilometers per hour as it passed through Naretha with its tiny collection of fettlers' huts. I was gazing out the window when I felt a sharp jolt, followed by abrupt shaking. I thought the train was negotiating some rough track but suitcases and bags started tumbling from the overhead racks.

The shaking continued for a few seconds before the train screeched to a halt and our carriage lurched to one side. It was leaning about 30 degrees from the vertical and when I looked out the window the ground appeared a long way down. I heard shouts from other compartments and a young child screamed. Our group joined the crowd gingerly making its way down the sloping corridor to the end of the carriage. Reaching the open door I leaped down and landed with a thud. The fierce outside heat was a rude shock after the train's air-conditioning.

People huddled in small groups, trying to understand what had happened. There was no shade, except that provided by the leaning carriages. I had some barley sugar that someone once told me calmed nerves so I offered it around before joining the other YMCA guys, who were staring up at the front half of the train a couple of hundred meters away. The back half, in which our carriage was the third of eight, lay on its side like a string of fallen dominoes. Everyone was mystified how two carriages could have separated, especially when the train was going at a modest speed on straight track. Just then one of our youngest members came running up.

"You should see what's happened in the dining car," he exclaimed. "Lights were shattered, cups and saucers smashed and tables upset. Everything's covered in dust. I saw one woman who'd been injured. It was really terrible."

Just then our group leader came striding towards us. He'd been talking to railway officials and gestured to us to come closer.

"You lads OK?" he asked as he approached us. "Everyone accounted for?"

A quick nod of heads confirmed that none of us had suffered any injury or was missing.

"It seems that we might have been lucky," he said. "A sandbank on the other side of the track probably prevented the derailed carriages from rolling over."

For the first time it dawned on me that we might have escaped a much greater disaster. While the initial derailed carriages lay skewed across the track, ours and the one behind were lying on their sides. The next two were down the embankment and the final two were off the rails. The rear observation car was on such a steep angle that passengers had to walk down the wall of the coach to get out.

We stood solemnly contemplating our situation and swatting flies. There was a lot of activity near the front of the train but railway staff prevented us going there. We could only wait until we received instructions how to proceed and comfort those who needed it.

After about half an hour a conductor approached and indicated to passengers from the back half of the train to gather around. He explained that staff and passengers had been injured but he spared us the details. We later learned that chefs preparing afternoon tea and soup for dinner were scalded and the heavy white china was smashed to smithereens. Injured passengers were being taken to the front of the train and when they were settled the rest of us were to follow with our luggage. The now much-shortened train would proceed to Kalgoorlie, the nearest town 320 kilometers away.

"We know this is going to be a squeeze," said the conductor, "but in light of the circumstances we ask your forbearance and cooperation." Then he turned to our group and added, "You YMCA lads can go in the luggage van next to the engine."

While that seemed a fairly daunting prospect, it was preferable to hanging around Naretha in the blazing sun. But when we discovered the luggage van wasn't air-conditioned we had second thoughts. Furthermore, with the additional luggage of half the train's 250 passengers it was extremely cramped. We felt like sheep crammed into a road train. After three hours at Naretha we felt a shudder as the train limped into action.

As we headed into the setting sun my thoughts turned to home and meeting my family the next day. What would I tell them? How much would they have heard about the accident? Surely it would have been on radio and television and probably in the Sunday paper if it hadn't gone to press before word of the derailment seeped through. Although our family didn't receive the paper our neighbors did and they would have told my parents if there was any news about the accident.

My parents did hear about it, but not as I anticipated. On Saturday night they had gone to play cards with friends. One of those friends awoke early the next morning, read the front-page story of the accident, and phoned my parents.

"Don't worry, Joyce," she said, "it says in the paper the YMCA boys are OK."

"What on earth are you talking about?" asked my mother.

"The train accident. On the Nullarbor. You haven't heard?"

My mother's heart sank. I'd been away several weeks and except for two postcards she hadn't heard from me.

"You said that John was due back today, so we figured he would've been on this train," said her friend. "Some weird accident happened on the Nullarbor. The train split in two and the back half went off the rails. Anyway, none of the YMCA boys was injured, so don't get upset. I bet John'll have a few stories to tell when he gets home."

As soon as my mother put down the phone there was a knock at the back door. Our neighbor stood there with the paper in hand, not knowing how to break the news. When my mother glanced at the headlines, she gasped. ONE KILLED WHEN EIGHT CARS DERAILED. Her friend hadn't told her the whole story.

A 70-year-old man had just left the dining car to return to his compartment. As he approached the carriage door a young man opened it for him to go through. As the older man crossed to the next carriage the two coaches came apart and he was thrown onto the track and killed. While the front of the train sailed ahead the latter half jumped the rails and tilted over before the automatic brakes kicked in. The young man who'd witnessed the gruesome spectacle managed to avert another tragedy when he grabbed a small girl who had been thrown down the corridor towards the open door.

It wasn't until I read Monday morning's paper that the severity of it all hit me. Splashed across the front page were the headlines EXPRESS LEAVES RAILS, MAN DIES, along with two large photographs of the strewn carriages. They were much more dramatic than the two photos I took with my tiny Kodak camera. Although the article went into considerable detail it offered no explanation about the cause of the derailment. The most probable theory was that excessive heat caused distortion of the line. But the reason for the uncoupling remained a mystery, which a board of inquiry that investigated the incident was never able to solve.

The journey to Kalgoorlie took longer than anticipated and when we arrived just before midnight ambulances and police thronged the station. Two doctors and a nurse who were passengers on the train had been tending the injured for nearly eight hours. Some had suspected spinal injuries, one an injured arm, and another suffered burns. Once they had been whisked away to the local hospital the rest of us were ushered to the Westland Express on the other side of the platform for the last leg of our long, and now tragic, journey. When we reached Perth the following afternoon photographers and reporters crowded the platform, along with anxious friends and relatives. Among them were my parents, sister and neighbors. My mother hugged me and began to cry; my father shook my hand. They pounded me with questions, which I tried to answer but found myself coming up short.

But one thing was sure. Like all of us who had posed for a group photo on this same platform a month before, I was a now a very different person. As time passed I began to view the experience as a rite of passage from childhood to adulthood. I was 13 and hadn't spent much time away from my family. The trip exposed me to different parts of Australia, taught me to manage on my own, and confronted me with life's contingency. It also impacted me in another way. Traveling with a group of teenage boys had awakened me to the world of male sexuality. It would take another 20 years and a whole different culture for me to fully grasp the significance of that and pursue it to its logical conclusion.

* * *

On the day of my departure from Calcutta I arrived at Howrah station an hour and a half early. Since I had a reserved berth I decided to head to the station cafeteria for a cup of chai and a samosa before boarding. When I returned to the platform 45 minutes later the crowd had grown enormously. So too had the yelling and screaming by impatient passengers, opportunistic porters and ever-hopeful salesmen. My ticket said my carriage and seat was I-19, so I tried to locate it by starting at one end of the train and making my way to the other. However, the numbers were scribbled on the side of the carriages in chalk and on some carriages they had been changed several times, resulting in a blurry smudge. What's more, the alphabetical numbering of the carriages wasn't sequential. I found carriages H and J but no I. I looked up at the station clock. Only 25 minutes remained before departure.

Battling the crowd, I gathered my luggage and walked the entire length of the train again, sure that I would find my carriage this time. Alas, I didn't. How could it not be there? Did I have a ticket for the wrong day or the wrong train? I was sure neither was the case. The station clock now showed less than 20 minutes to go. I urgently needed to speak with a conductor but trying to get near one would require a substantial athletic feat. The situation was growing more desperate by the minute. Tossing politeness aside, I barreled my way through the crowd surrounding one conductor, ignoring several unsavory comments as I clawed my way through.

"Conductor sahib," I shouted. "Please help me. I've gone up and down the train twice and I can't find my carriage. Where is I-19?"

With finely honed bureaucratic nonchalance the conductor ignored my plea and continued what he was doing. I repeated myself, louder.

"Can't you see I'm busy?" he retorted. "Wait your turn."

"But conductor sahib, the train is about to leave!"

I thrust my hand in front of him and waved my ticket back and forth. The clock was ticking; my stomach tightening. Then he suddenly turned towards me and grabbed the ticket from my hand. Glancing at it he stated bluntly, "This is down the other end of the train. You'll have to hurry."

This felt like progress but it was now seven minutes to scheduled departure time, and in spite of their dismal record of arriving on time Indian trains were prone to leave on time. Mustering every ounce of energy I could, I grabbed my bags and made a wild dash down the platform. Bystanders shot me puzzled looks. What was this crazy foreigner up to? Was he being chased? Had he overdosed? I ran the length of the platform, dodging bodies and animals, tea stands and banana-wallahs. Nearing the end of the platform I heard the first of two whistles. I had to get on this train. I tried paying attention to the chalk marks near the carriage doorways but still saw nothing that looked like an 'I'.

The second whistle blew. It was now or never. This section of the train was first class, for which I could not afford a ticket, even if by some rare miracle a seat were available. First-class berths were much more expensive and usually booked well in advance. Desperate to catch the train, I jumped into the nearest carriage and dropped my bag inside the door. A strange mixture of anger, stupidity and powerlessness overcame me. How could I have arrived at the station 90 minutes before and ended up like this?

When a conductor eventually appeared 40 minutes later, I showed him my ticket and tried to explain my situation. His eyes squinted and his brow furrowed.

"This is not a first-class ticket," he exclaimed. "Your carriage is far from here. You will have to wait until we reach Jamshedpur and I will take you. But you'll need to be quick because we only stop for a few minutes. We will be arriving in about an hour. Wait here."

I plunked down on the floor and contemplated my situation. It had been such a good couple of weeks fundraising in Calcutta. For once, things seemed to be going my way. Surely my luck would continue a bit longer. But India had an uncanny way of raising you to great heights one moment then knocking you down the next. It was something my logical mind could never fathom and over which I had no control. My life felt like an accordion, splayed apart one moment and squished together the next. Yet something about this concertinaed lifestyle was strangely energizing. Right now my body and mind were in overdrive, so I tried to calm myself with the rolling motion of the train as it sped west.

It was just after 11 o'clock when the train pulled into Jamshedpur station. All I could see was the dimly lit platform against a pitch-black sky. In the distance a dog's bark broke the silence. As the train came to a halt the conductor appeared and gestured to me to follow him. Our carriage was beyond the end of the platform, leaving a sizable gap between the bottom step and the ground. The conductor jumped down and I passed him my luggage before leaping myself.

"Hurry up!" he commanded, as he led the way at a brisk trot. The train seemed to have lengthened since Howrah station. The first whistle blew and the conductor motioned to me to go faster. With my heavy case I could barely keep up with him. Just as the second whistle blew he pointed to a carriage door and motioned me to get up. I glanced up to where the carriage number was meant to be. There was only a chalky smudge.

As I tried to catch my breath the conductor began checking seat numbers. When he reached 19 it was occupied. Given the hour, I was not surprised when its occupant reacted angrily to being awoken and asked to show his ticket. The conductor entered into a heated exchange with the irate passenger, drawing a crowd of onlookers, some of whom took sides, while others offered advice. I wanted to shrivel up and disappear.

With a thunderous voice the conductor ordered the man out of the berth and told me to take it. The look on the conductor's face suggested he would be glad to see the backs of both of us. Any notion I had of my rights had been displaced by a gnawing sense of guilt. I had emerged the victor, but at a price. The departing passenger glared at me and muttered something under his breath. I was exhausted and just wanted to sleep.

My berth was a lower one parallel to the direction of the train, next to the door at the end of the carriage. If I'd known this when I bought the ticket I would've asked for another berth, but given I had only done so a week before departure, posing as a tourist to avail myself of the limited tourist quota, I couldn't argue. There was no space for my luggage in the overhead racks, so I had to put it under my seat. As I did an older man from the compartment opposite came over.

"You should be careful putting your case so close to the door," he said. "It would be easy for someone to take it. You can store it with us if you like."

I was a taken aback by his offer and hesitated for a second or two. Was it genuine or was it a ruse to get his hands on my luggage? Train travel in India had taught me to keep my luggage within sight and hand's reach at all times. I thanked the man but said I would prefer to keep it close to me. He looked at me askance, shrugged his shoulders, and returned to his compartment. But his advice wasn't entirely wasted. I stowed the case under the berth at the end farthest from the door. As I did, I was reminded how heavy it was with printers' blocks, jars of pickles, and my beloved shortwave radio among other things. Its weight alone was a disincentive for any light-fingered intruder.

Despite all I'd been through, it took me a while to get to sleep. The train stopped several times during the night, and each time I reached down under my berth to check on my case. But in the early hours of the morning I must have dozed off. Only after Kalyan, the last stop before Bombay, I woke up. I was surprised so many people were moving about the carriage, since usually the slightest noise or movement awakens me.

Instinctively, I lowered my hand and waved it around. Nothing was there. I rolled over and looked beneath my berth. There was a gaping space. I wanted to scream "No!" It couldn't be true. How was it possible that someone had taken my case from right under me? Thank goodness I'd put my money and passport in my satchel under my pillow.

While I was still trying to grasp what had happened, the man from the compartment opposite came over and sat down. He was sympathetic to my plight but with an "I-told-you-so" look in his eye. For a brief moment I wondered if he might have had something to do with my case's disappearance. But that was absurd. He invited me to join his family for chai and insisted I put my remaining luggage with theirs, even though we were only a short distance from Bombay. I gladly complied.

As the train snaked its way through the outlying areas of the city the suffocating heat of the lower elevation engulfed me. I watched the early morning pageant of people bathing and defecating, but could only think of the loss of my case and how I would break the news to my colleagues.

Instead of wallowing in self-pity I resolved to do something. When the train pulled into Victoria Terminus I went straight to the railway police and lodged a complaint for stolen property. The duty officer didn't blink an eyelid as I related my tale of woe. He must have heard thousands of stories like it, especially from naïve foreigners.

"You do one thing," he ordered. "Fill out this form and sign it."

He pushed a yellowing piece of paper in front of me. It looked to be the same form some punctilious British civil servant had designed a couple of centuries before. Filling it out was futile. It would end up in a file that over time would be shredded by rats or cockroaches in some moldy storage room. But it created the illusion I was doing something to address my sorry situation.

As I scribbled on the piece of paper I began to reflect on the events of the last 24 hours. First the debacle trying to find the carriage, then the confrontation with the person who had taken my berth, and now this. Were they connected? Did the person I ousted from the berth steal back in the early hours of the morning and exact his revenge? Or was I just the unfortunate victim of an opportunistic theft that happened hundreds of times a day on Indian trains? As I mulled over these questions, I remembered a pendant of St. Christopher, the patron saint of travelers, that an Australian friend had sent me. I'd put it in a drawer and forgotten about it. As soon as I arrived home I vowed to take it out and wear it from now on.

But I was still not ready to face my colleagues. An odd mix of shame and guilt overcame me. I needed to rehearse my story and compose myself. I headed for the station dining room and ordered my favorite 'full breakfast' — a hangover from British times that could still be found in some Indian railway stations. Between the imitation cornflakes and greasy fried eggs I couldn't hold back the tears. They began as a trickle but within moments I was sobbing. I couldn't remember when I had ever wept like this. I was embarrassed others would notice but few people were in the room. As I reached into my pocket and pulled out my handkerchief I pushed my plate away and let the tears take their course. India had triumphed once again.

FLYING NIGERIA
ERRWAYS

· · · · ·

If I believed in omens I never would have taken this trip. From the outset several co-workers questioned its value. Helping our Nigerian colleagues secure a major grant for a village health project was exactly the kind of thing our International Development and Funding Team had been set up to do. But the expense involved and the difficulty finding a partner to accompany me to West Africa were just two of many obstacles. After numerous phone calls we learned that the director of our UK office could spare a week, although he would arrive a couple of days after me.

On 6th March 1987, the night before I was to take the boat to London to catch my flight to Nigeria, a cross-channel ferry capsized off the Belgian coast, killing 193 passengers and crew. Was this a warning? Should I back down? Such questions unsettled me but not enough to thwart my efforts to get to West Africa. I took the hydrofoil instead and arrived in London in good time to catch my plane. But as I walked up to the Nigeria Airways counter at Heathrow airport my heart sank. On the monitor were the words 'Flight Canceled.' I waited several minutes for the ticketing agent to look up from his computer. When he continued to ignore me, I cleared my throat to announce my presence.

"Excuse me sir, is it Flight 374 to Lagos that's canceled?"

"Of course," he replied, eyes still glued to the screen.

"I see. Why is it canceled?"

"They've sent the plane to Brussels for repairs."

Was this some kind of joke? I'd just come from Brussels. I would have thought any repairs could have been handled here at one of the world's major airports, but better the plane being repaired in Brussels than falling to pieces in mid-air. I glanced at my watch. It was 7:30 pm. I had last eaten at midday, anticipating a meal on the flight.

"When do you expect the plane to be ready?" I asked.

"Don't know."

"So what am I to do?"

His eyes communicated volumes. It was that old, familiar 'Why bother me, I just work here' look. After further encouragement I managed to extract a verbal reply.

"Go see the station manager."

"And where do I find him?"

"First floor, room 306."

Lugging my suitcase, I trudged to the opposite end of the terminal, up a flight of stairs and down a narrow corridor. Room 306 was hard to miss. A long line of passengers spewed out its door and snaked down the passageway. I sighed as I added myself to its tail. I desperately wanted something to eat but dared not leave in case the manager should appear. About an hour later, a tall, dark figure materialized and made his way into the office. Dressed in a traditional, loose-fitting white shirt and pants with a matching white cap, he reeked of importance as he strode past the gawking crowd.

Without offering any explanation or apology he plunked himself down at his desk and was besieged by irate passengers. Poking my head through the door, I gleaned that most were demanding to have their tickets endorsed over to another airline or be given a hotel room for the night. One by one they all managed to get something out of the beleaguered man. Finally it was my turn. He glanced at my ticket and shook his head.

"This is an excursion ticket. There's nothing I can do with it."

I sensed he was right, knowing that we always chose the lowest fares and had bought the ticket at the last minute. However, I was not about to concede defeat right away. This called for other tactics, the first of which was to plead on humanitarian grounds.

"Excuse me, sir, but I am working on a community health project in the Niger delta and have an important appointment with your Health Minster the day after tomorrow. It's critical I get to Lagos immediately."

"As I said, there's nothing I can do. The plane is still being repaired. I don't know when it will be ready to fly."

I decided to increase the pressure.

"But I'm not responsible for the flight being canceled. That's your problem and it's your job to find a solution. You signed other passengers over to British Caledonian so you should do the same for me."

"I've already told you. Your ticket doesn't allow me to do it. Besides, it's non-refundable."

"But you are the station manager. Are you telling me that you don't have the authority to make decisions like this?

I folded my arms, glared at him, and issued an ultimatum.

"I'm not leaving this office until you sign over my ticket!"

I have no idea where these words came from. They seemed to fly out of my mouth without my consent. I didn't usually demand the impossible. But now I'd spoken I couldn't back down. I had to maintain my bullying front, or look a complete fool. We went around the same track several times. Finally, he stood up abruptly and left the room. I was sure I had lost the battle but to my utter surprise he returned shortly after, sat down without looking at me, and scribbled on my ticket.

"I shouldn't be doing this," he confessed. "British Caledonian might not even accept it."

I sat and watched, barely able to contain my delight. When he handed me the ticket I thanked him profusely and left quickly before he changed his mind.

Like the rest of the terminal, the departure hall was deserted except for the odd backpacker stretched out over several seats. I looked at the indicator board for my flight but couldn't find it. Other passengers had told me that it was scheduled to leave at 11:00 the next morning. Then I remembered that British Caledonian flew out of Gatwick airport and I was at Heathrow.

Since I had nearly 12 hours to make the trip across London I wasn't unduly bothered by this. I was much more concerned about my stomach that was crying out for attention. But every vendor at Heathrow had shut down for the night. Victoria Station seemed my best bet. Surely this hub of London's rail system would have places open around the clock. Since I had to go there to catch a train to Gatwick it was an obvious choice. My instincts proved correct, although the choices of fare at Victoria Station at one in the morning were somewhat limited. A cheese and tomato sandwich and a cup of milky tea never tasted so good.

Next morning when I checked in at British Caledonian's ticket counter at Gatwick I nervously handed the agent my ticket. I was severely sleep-deprived and sure there would be a problem. Had the Nigeria Airways manager only pretended to endorse my ticket over? Had he duped me into believing that I had beaten him down? The agent screwed up his eyes and took his time reading the overwritten ticket. Seconds seemed like minutes.

"I can't believe they endorsed this ticket over to us," he declared. "They've lost its total value. You're one lucky man."

My mind flashed back to watching Malcolm McDowell, the aspiring young coffee salesman in the film *O Lucky Man!* Did such absurdities portrayed in that movie happen in real life? As I pondered the question pangs of guilt began to nag at me. I had bullied my way into something I wasn't entitled to and was bound to get my comeuppance. But my overriding concern at that moment was to get on a plane to Lagos.

"Serves them bloody well right," I said to myself as I headed to the gate.

Once I boarded the aircraft I was lulled into a false sense of security that everything was going to be OK. Familiar British accents and the aroma of freshly brewing coffee assured me I was in good hands. I had phoned our London office to let them know my change of plans and asked them to notify colleagues in Lagos that I would be coming on this later flight. Just before we took off, the captain announced a minor failure in the hydraulic system that would need to be taken care of. Three hours, a movie, and lunch later our plane lifted off. Nearly 30 hours after leaving Brussels I was on my way to Africa.

Apart from the cheap fare, the other reason I chose Nigeria Airways was that its flight arrived in Lagos in the morning, whereas British Caledonian arrived in the evening. Colleagues had warned me about the dangers of traveling between the airport and the city at night. As it turned out, the British

Caledonian flight landed about 9:30 pm. I prayed someone might be there to meet me. Given the change of flight and subsequent delay my chances of being met seemed slim. I wasn't relishing taking a taxi at this time of night into a strange city in a country I'd never set foot in. I went through customs and immigration without any hassle but then noticed a large sign that said all visitors were required to change a minimum of US$100 into Nigerian naira. I didn't have a hundred US dollars, since I was expecting to be taken care of by my hosts while in the country. I waited a few minutes until a large crowd amassed around the currency exchange then made a dash for the exit.

Just as I did I heard something that sounded like my name over the public address system. My heart soared. Ignoring an airport official who kept pointing me in the direction of the currency exchange, I made a run for the glass doors, behind which people were pushing and shouting at incoming passengers. I then spotted a man in gray suit waving a piece of paper with my name on it. I ran up to him, gave his hand a firm shake, and told him how pleased I was to see him. He may well have said the same to me. As we drove into Lagos he politely revealed that this was his third visit to the airport that day and that he had been there more than four hours this time.

* * *

The three jam-packed weeks I spent in West Africa more than offset the difficulty I had getting there. In Nigeria I was hosted by one of the country's senior bankers, put up at his luxurious guest house, chauffeur driven in his air-conditioned Mercedes 800 kilometers to the site of the proposed project, and warmly received by Nigeria's Minister of Health who promised us a $125,000 grant. I shook more hands with respectable old men than in the rest of my life combined. In neighboring Côte d'Ivoire, where we had a regional office, I pushed my French language skills to new limits, visited the world's largest basilica, and devoured bush rat stew prepared in my honor. Now it was time to return to London; the first leg of the journey was from Abidjan to Lagos.

When I entered the airline's office in Abidjan I felt conspicuous as the only non-African in the room. I presented my ticket to confirm my return flights and took a deep breath.

"I don't think there is a flight to London from Lagos on Saturday evening," said the young woman behind the counter.

"But your office in Lagos confirmed me on it two weeks ago."

"Well, sir, they don't always tell us when they change flights."

"Can you phone or telex Lagos to find out?"

"Sorry but the lines are down between here and Lagos."

"Well, just in case there is a flight, could you at least confirm my connection from Abidjan to Lagos?"

"Just a minute, sir," she said as she reached for a nearby phone.

"Hi Mavis, is that you? The evening flight to Lagos, did it fly last Saturday?"

I wondered what last week's flight had to do with this week's but then I reminded myself that this was West Africa, not Western Europe. Five minutes later she finished chatting with Mavis and assured me that my flight would be operating this week and I was confirmed on it. I had my doubts.

When I reached Abidjan airport my plane was nowhere to be seen. I checked in my case and waited over an hour, as more and more African women arrived carrying large bundles on their heads. Then without warning a plane appeared and pulled up at the main gate. I was expecting a boarding announcement, but none came. The mushrooming crowd surged through the terminal door, sweeping me along with it onto the tarmac and up the steps into the plane. Seat assignments, security checks and boarding by rows belonged to another world. It was survival of the fittest and fastest. I grabbed the first seat I could find and flopped down.

Being more experienced in the ways of West Africa than I, my hosts in Abidjan had given me a few provisions to tide me over, just in case things didn't go according to plan. I had two boiled eggs, three bananas, a bunch of carrot sticks and a thick paperback. I was expecting a layover of five to six hours in Lagos but on landing the airline staff assured me there was no flight to London that night, although there might be one the following morning, depending on the plane arriving from London and not needing repairs. I braced myself for another night at another airport.

Murtala Mohammed International Airport was one of the most spacious terminals I'd seen, with endless departure lounges dotted throughout its cavernous building. However, only a handful showed any sign of activity. It was a grandiose temple built to honor vanity and nationalism. A small snack bar and gift shop in the main departure hall accounted for the total commercial life of the airport. I had no trouble finding an empty bench in the transit lounge and decided to indulge in my highly coveted supplies. Just as I began eating, a harried-looking man appeared and headed in my direction.

"Your passport, sir."

"Beg your pardon," I muttered with a mouthful of boiled egg.

"You are staying here tonight?"

"I guess I am. My flight to London doesn't appear to be happening and I can't afford a hotel."

"Well, then, you must give me your passport."

"Give you my passport? Who are you?"

"I'm an immigration officer. Anyone who stays at the airport overnight must hand over their passport."

I looked at him more closely. Was he really an immigration officer or was he a con man? Foreign passports no doubt fetched a handy amount on the black market here.

"How do I know you are an immigration officer?" I asked.

He put his hand in his pocket and produced a crumpled old card with Government of Nigeria printed at the top.

"Why do you need my passport?"

"Many people stay in transit then abscond into Nigeria."

I assured the man that as much as it had been an unsurpassed privilege to be a guest in his great country I had little desire to remain here permanently, but he didn't seem persuaded. He shifted his weight from one foot to the other and clicked his knuckles. I felt I shouldn't push my luck any further and fumbled in my carry-on for my passport. Before I gave it to him I had one more question.

"When will I get my passport back? I'm flying to London in the morning."

"I will bring it to you."

Yes, I thought, for a small fee, no doubt. Handing over my passport was like cutting off one of my arms.

Finding an empty bench to sleep on wasn't a problem, but sleeping on it was. Apart from the hardness of the bench, I feared someone might try to rob me since I was the only person in the entire lounge. Sleep came in fits and starts.

Next morning I went to a washroom and splashed water on my face to revive my flagging spirits. As I returned to my bench the immigration officer reappeared and presented me with my passport. I was elated. I thanked him and asked where I might find my luggage, assuming it had made it from Abidjan the night before. He informed me that I could retrieve it from the Nigeria Airways counter but I would need to re-check it and go through customs and immigration.

I made my way to the check-in counter and explained my situation to an airline employee. After mulling around in a sea of luggage for several minutes he located my case and dragged it back to the counter. I was relieved to see it but wasn't expecting his next instruction.

"Open it."

"Here?" I asked. "I thought customs inspected luggage."

"No. We do it for them."

How strange, I thought, having airline staff act as customs officials. In all my travels I'd never come across such a thing, but seeing no alternative I did as he asked. He rifled through my case, throwing its carefully packed contents into complete disarray with an aggressiveness that seemed designed to underscore the power he held over me. I couldn't tell what he was looking for but he seemed disappointed.

"So what do you have for me?" he asked point blank.

I was blown away by his audacity. At least he's honest about it, I thought. Slapping my last few naira down in front of him, I repacked my case and watched it slip away on the conveyor belt, before I headed to Gate 25 where, with luck and fate coinciding, I would find a London-bound DC-10 waiting for me.

Before reaching the gate I had to go through exit immigration. Situated midway between check-in and the departure lounge, the booth stood in the middle of an empty concourse. I went up to the counter and presented my passport and ticket. The young man in the booth gave them a desultory look and glanced at me.

"Australian, ha? You have any Australian dollars?"

"Sorry, mate, they're not much use in these parts."

"US dollars?"

"Nope."

"British pounds?"

"No luck. And in case you're next question is naira, I just gave my last to your friend at the check-in counter."

The barest of smiles insinuated itself at the corner of his mouth, as he picked up his metal stamp and banged it down on a fresh page of my passport. I gathered my documents and headed down the concourse.

Gate 25 was not hard to find. It was the only one where people had gathered. As I sauntered up to the seating area, I looked at the sign behind the counter and gasped. The word 'London' was nowhere to be seen. All it said was Flight 278 to Rome via Kano. What happened to the London leg? Had they decided to drop it today? Was this a different flight? Would I have to spend another night at the airport?

I joined the burgeoning crowd around the counter and jostled my way to the front.

"Is this the flight to London?" I blurted.

The woman behind the counter ignored my question but several passengers assured me it was the London flight.

"They don't always bother to put it on the sign board," one of them said.

Around 11:30 am, without any announcement, passengers began boarding the plane. This time, surprisingly, there were seat assignments so I found my mine and settled down in anticipation of my first meal since leaving Abidjan the day before. When nothing materialized in the two-hour flight to Kano, I steeled myself to wait until the next leg, when we would have a full passenger load. An hour after we left the dusty plains of northern Nigeria, flight attendants appeared pushing squeaking carts down the aisles and issued what looked like war rations — boiled chicken, white rice, and a glass of water, which I demolished in minutes. Little did I know it would be my last food or drink before London.

Just before we touched down in Rome, the overhead monitors, which had been blank throughout the flight, came alive with a crackle as we were presented with the local television news. I couldn't tell whether this was a distraction to take our minds off the shaky landing or an attempt to provide some form of entertainment. I did wonder how many Nigerians, who were the bulk of passengers, could follow the Italian newsreader.

When we finally landed at Heathrow I was overcome with relief. I was back in the realm of the familiar. After I disembarked down the jetway, I came face to face with the Nigeria Airways station manager with whom I had locked horns the night of my departure four weeks before. Dressed in the same white cap and flowing robes, he greeted passengers with a robust handshake and gleeful smile...until he saw me. I nodded politely and made a hasty exit.

After waiting more than half an hour to go through immigration, I made straight for the nearest food stall and ordered the all-day breakfast and a large cup of coffee. As soon as I finished eating I headed for the Underground to catch the train to the city. But when I reached the airport station I had just missed the last train. I resigned myself to spending my second consecutive night, and my third for the trip, at an airport. By now I was an old pro at the game. I pulled out my inflatable pillow, dossed down in the nearest corner, and went to sleep.

* * *

Shortly after returning to Brussels I was reading the *International Herald Tribune* when a headline caught my eye: 'Ailing Nigeria Airways: A Case for Privatization?' Among the litany of complaints about the airline was that it was not unusual for schedules and destinations to be ignored, for reservations not to be honored, and for meals to go unserved. It was the only carrier in the 125-member International Air Transport Association that had been suspended for non-payment of dues and it did not produce a profit-and-loss sheet. Its policy of keeping air fares artificially low and serving destinations with too few passengers were given as reasons for its financial malaise. In the same paper Reuters reported that a French airline maintenance company had obtained a court order to prevent a Nigeria Airways Airbus from leaving France because the airline owed more than $20 million for repairs to its planes, in one instance due to a crash landing. This left only one Airbus operational out of the four it owned.

In May 2003 the company went into liquidation with debts of $60 million. Later that year an inquiry into alleged corruption in the company reported that the Nigerian government had demanded the return of a missing $400 million. Among those ordered to return money included two ex-ministers and several former officials. One minister allegedly sold two planes without authorization. Eventually a new airline was set up to replace Nigeria Airways, which was dubbed by many a disgruntled passenger as 'Nigeria Airwaste' and 'Nigeria Errways.'

Some years after my trek to West Africa I was leaving an airport in the United States when I noticed a sign posted at the entry to the departure lounge. It read: 'Attention: Passengers are advised that the Secretary of Transportation has determined that the following airports do not maintain and administer effective aviation security measures. Murtala Mohammed International, Lagos and Port-au-Prince International, Haiti.' Was I surprised? I walked past the sign with a smug 'been there, done that (and survived)' look on my face. The US Federal Aviation Administration suspended all air service between Lagos and the United States in 1993 and didn't resume it until 2001. The British government also suspended the air link between London and Lagos from 1998 to 2001.

During the late 1980s and 1990s the international terminal became a dangerous place. Travelers were harassed both inside and outside the terminal by criminals and airport staff. Immigration officers required bribes before stamping passports, while customs agents demanded payment for nonexistent fees. Amid a spate of tarmac robberies, thieves placed rocks and logs in front of a plane on the taxiway as it prepared to depart. Passengers watched in dismay as the robbers broke open the cargo hold and made off with luggage.

I might not have taken much notice of these reports had it not been for a dinner conversation I had one night in 1995 with a friend and her colleagues in Guatemala. I happened to mention the night I spent in the Mohammed Murtala International transit lounge. This brought an immediate reaction from one of the women. She told of a co-worker who was taken to a private room on the pretext of having her passport examined and found herself the victim of an attempted rape. She managed to flee the room and fling herself into the arms of the first Westerner she encountered.

Fortunately, things have improved substantially in recent years. Following President Olusegun Obasanjo's democratic election in 1999, airport security was greatly enhanced. Police instituted a shoot-on-sight policy for anyone found in the secure areas, which brought a halt to cargo robberies. Malfunctioning infrastructure was repaired, the entire airport was cleaned, and new restaurants and duty-free stores were opened. Bilateral agreements between Nigeria and other countries were revived and new ones signed. Perhaps one day I may return to Nigeria, but if I do I'm glad I won't have to fly with Nigeria Errways.

MAYBE, BUT NOT YET

. . . . .

Before we left on our trip to Indonesia in 2012 I practiced Bahasa Indonesian every day. Compared to other languages it seemed easy. I memorized lists of items, critical sentences like 'Where's the toilet?' and the odd bit of flattery. But I soon discovered that only three expressions were really important — *tidak apa apa* (no problem), *mungkin* (maybe) and *belum* (not yet). In this country of 273 million people, 300 ethnic groups and more than 700 languages 'getting along' is not just a necessity but a way of life. Confrontation is assiduously avoided and anger is frowned upon. Saying no is a no-no. As the German author Horst Henry Geerken noted after 18 years in Indonesia, "the highest virtue is always to remain calm and collected. Impatience and haste are regarded as indecorous."

Coming from the United States with its daily barrages of political invectives, mass shootings and media mudslinging we found this a refreshing change. It more than compensated for Indonesia's intense heat and humidity. During our month in the country, Bruce, my husband, and I divided our time between Bali and Lombok. With its rich cultural traditions that have survived the onslaught of mass tourism Bali is the senior partner. As one of our Lombok friends pointed out, "You can see Bali from Lombok, but you can't see Lombok from Bali." Sadly Lombok is showing all the signs of emulating its neighbor but hopefully without the accompanying traffic snarls, lagging infrastructure and environmental degradation.

Having grown up in Australia I was aware of Bali's lure for travelers, especially from the 1960s onward when intrepid backpackers, dope-smoking hippies and sun-scorched surfers discovered this largely untainted paradise at their doorstep. But having lived outside Australia most of my adult life I wasn't aware that these early forays had grown into something much grander. From Western Australia alone nearly 400,000 people holiday in Bali each year. Not surprising then, that when the Bali terrorist bombings occurred in 2002, 88 of the 202 killed were Australians.

But our choice of destination was more personal. A school friend, Megan, and her husband, Grahaem, had visited Bali over many years and supported an Indonesian family running a B&B in Ubud, the island's cultural hub. When she suggested we pay them a visit, we couldn't resist.

* * *

Both islands are indescribably beautiful with their iridescent green rice paddies, towering volcanoes and postcard-perfect beaches. But what captures most outsiders about Bali and Lombok is the warm, gentle nature of the people. With an innate politeness, butter-melting smiles and an ever-present sense of humor, they make visitors feel immediately welcome. They also have a strong devotion to family, a deep respect for age, and a reverence for cultural traditions.

Few people embodied these qualities as clearly as Ketut Suarsa, owner of Bali Breeze Bungalows in Ubud. Ketut, or 'Pak' as he was affectionately called (short for 'Bapak' or 'father'), is a guru of all things Balinese. As we were driving from the airport I mentioned Miguel Corvarrubius, a Mexican artist-cum-ethnologist who spent time in Bali in the 1930s and wrote a celebrated book about the island. Ketut's eyes lit up at the mention of the name. The next day he presented me with a new copy of this expensive publication.

"This has everything you need to know about Bali. Please have it." he said. It felt like an assignment of biblical proportions.

In his late sixties, Ketut wore many hats. During our short stay he acted as manager, driver, guide, ticket purchaser, raconteur and above all, friend. When we left it felt like saying goodbye to a beloved uncle. While conversing his rounded face would take on an animated expression as he launched into a subject, be it a myth from the Ramayana or a tirade against some unscrupulous practice that he would dismiss disparagingly as 'monkey business'.

One day Ketut took us to the village of Tenganan, home of Bali's original Aga people in eastern Bali. We walked for hours through verdant rice paddies and lush jungle. Even though a motor cycle accident had left him with a slight limp, Ketut set a challenging pace. Wearing only thongs he led us along narrow paths, over irrigation canals and down a steep canyon during the hottest part of the day. When we stopped for lunch at local restaurant he declined to join us, but sat at an adjoining table. At first we were disappointed but then remembered that except for festivals and ceremonies, eating is usually a solitary exercise for Balinese.

On another occasion we wished we'd had Ketut to guide us. We were visiting the famed rice terraces of Jatiwulih, a UNESCO World Heritage site, whose winding valleys of intensely green fields are a feast for the eyes. Our driver dropped us at a gravel pathway with the instructions, "Go straight until you come to a path on the right. Take it up the hill to the restaurant. I'll meet you there." It sounded simple enough. We set off at a fair clip, passing farmers working their fields and cows tethered to stakes. When we hadn't sighted a path after half an hour we asked other walkers. They confirmed we were on the right track but needed to descend to a river and come to a temple, from where we would find the road back to the restaurant.

After several more conversations we found the river and the temple, but no path. Bruce was convinced we were going farther away from our destination. Traipsing along muddy trails and over irrigation canals, we headed up to the nearest ridge. When we arrived at a vantage point we spotted a building far in the distance. Could that be the restaurant? Rain clouds were gathering, we hadn't eaten since breakfast, and it was now late afternoon. We kept climbing to the top of another ridge where we discovered a gravel road, so followed that for a couple more kilometers. As we turned a corner we came upon a road crew who assured us we were close to our destination. When we finally reached the restaurant and located our driver he had that 'I've-seen-it-all-before' look in his eyes.

Our arrival in Bali coincided with the Galungan festival in which families welcome ancestors back home with feasting and prayers at the family temple. For several days women wove delicate offerings from coconut fronds and men carved long bamboo poles known as penjors that lined every street. On the day itself Nyoman, the assistant manager of Bali Breeze, arrived bearing Balinese sarongs for us to wear. He informed us that Ketut wanted us to dress appropriately for this special occasion. With Nyoman's help we donned our new attire and headed into town, where we received many compliments from Balinese but strange looks from foreigners.

As we strolled around Ubud we noticed many young men washing their motor cycles. At first we thought this was another Galungan activity but later learned that it was a common practice. Indonesians own more than 40 million motor cycles, about 75% of all vehicles in the country. They drive them with and without helmets, on all sides of the road, and weave in and out of traffic like slalom skiers. In some parts of the world this would make for chaos and accidents. With tooting horns and an ingrained politeness, Indonesian motorcyclists negotiate traffic like they do everything else — in a most accommodating way. Those who own larger vehicles lavish similar care on them. As one driver exclaimed, "My wife says I'm married to my car. But how can I help it? I spend more of my life with it than I do with her!"

You aren't in Bali long before you notice that everything is an art form — the elegant presentation of food on your plate, the exquisite offerings to the gods that appear at your doorstep every morning, the interior walls in family compounds that are built to confuse intruding demons. Art surrounds you, even when you least expect it. Standing at a urinal in an airport toilet I found myself gazing into an aquarium of tropical fish; above the wash basins was an arrangement of fragrant frangipani flowers. At first this penchant for the artistic seemed strange but it soon began to affect us. In Balinese society creativity of any sort is deeply honored. Being a painter, carver, dancer, musician or actor is regarded with high esteem. You may be a taxi driver or school teacher by day and a Wali dancer or gamelan player by night. The latter are not peripheral to everyday life, but central to it.

An opportunity to create our own art form was a cooking class in Ubud. Along with two young Brits and a French woman, we showed up one morning at the Bumbu Bali restaurant to be greeted by Wayan, chef and teacher. After visiting the nearby market to familiarize ourselves with local herbs, spices, fruit and vegetables, we returned to the restaurant to begin the first of seven dishes. They ranged from base gede, the essential Balinese spice paste, to pork sate, sweet tempe and chicken stew. Each of us took turns in creating a dish under Wayan's watchful eye and beaming smile. He insisted we use our sense of taste to tell when the food was 'right' and that we finish each plate with an appropriate garnish. After consuming all seven of our creations, plus a complimentary dessert, we left Bumbu Bali a little wiser and significantly heavier than when we arrived.

We ate many delicious meals during our month in Indonesia but two stand out. If guests stay more than a week, Ketut treats them to a sumptuous Balinese feast of meat, vegetable, tofu and rice dishes. Since we had taken a Balinese cooking class, the chef agreed to let us help her, although she scrutinized us closely and did the lion's share of the work. When everything was ready she proudly displayed the food for us and our friends, but as splendid as it was it felt sacrilegious to destroy its artful arrangement.

The other memorable meal was in very different circumstances. It was a stormy day and we had driven across the island to Singaraja, the former Dutch colonial capital on the north coast. By early afternoon we were starving, so our driver suggested we check out some fish warungs at the beach. On the way we became trapped behind a funeral procession that slowed us down to a snail's pace and made us even more ravenous. When we finally arrived at the beach it appeared deserted and the wind was blowing furiously. Finding a place to eat seemed out of the question.

Then our driver spotted someone cooking fresh tuna in a lean-to kitchen and asked if she would prepare food for us. Within minutes we were presented with plate-size steaks of grilled tuna, bowls of water spinach, spicy salads and heaps of rice, the centerpiece of any Balinese meal. Words like 'fresh' and 'feast' took on a whole new meaning. Protected from raging winds by a flimsy cloth awning, we sat cross-legged in the sand at a low table in a thatched shelter. Using only our right hand as custom demands, we indulged in this magnificent spread. When we finished the meal, the bill came to US$9 for the three of us.

Two weeks in Bali passed quickly. When it was time for our friends to return to Australia, Bruce and I headed to Lombok. What would it be like, this predominantly Islamic island, after the genteel Hindu-Buddhist-animist Bali? We were warned about possible hassles by taxi drivers and boatmen and a higher incidence of petty crime. In contrast to Bali's prosperity fueled by years of tourist income, Lombok was regarded as the poorer cousin. But many of these fears and stereotypes were dispelled as we came to know and love Lombok. People were warm, receptive, helpful, and like most Indonesians always good for a laugh. As Horst Henry Geerken put it, "there is no such thing as a humorless Indonesian."

* * *

Like Ketut in Bali, one person was pivotal to our time in Lombok. Balinese with Dutch ancestry, Herman was a guide for a German visitor. We met on the island of Gili Gede off southwest Lombok and quickly became friends. With 400 inhabitants spread over four fishing villages, the island takes about six hours to walk around. Keen to meet the locals, Bruce and I decided to give it a go. As we inflicted our limited Bahasa Indonesian on them, the villagers practiced their basic English on us, while offering us food, drink and cigarettes. In one village we met a group of women chatting animatedly as they prepared food and watched over children. One took a fancy to my sunglasses and gestured that she'd like to try them on. Wanting to pay her a compliment, I dug into my sketchy phrasebook memory and came up with *merangsang*. The women shrieked with laughter. When I later checked I found that its meanings varied from 'exciting' and 'stimulating' to 'sexy' and 'hot'.

Throughout our four weeks in Indonesia many things impressed us and called us to question some of our own cultural assumptions. Wherever we went we never heard a child cry or scream. From birth until about two, children are regarded as gifts of the gods and are not allowed to touch the ground, lest it contaminate them. They are carried by parents or siblings until they are old enough to join other children and are then allowed to roam as they please. There is little concern for their safety, since siblings, older children and the entire community take care of them. Visitors to Indonesia have commented that children seem to mature early, perhaps in part because of these child-rearing practices.

Before leaving Gili Gede we tried booking accommodation in Kuta, a beach resort on Lombok's southern coast. Every place we phoned was full, which was puzzling since it was low season. Then Herman remembered that the annual Nyale festival was taking place in Kuta. We were visiting on the one day of the year when people from all over Lombok descended on the town. Nevertheless, we decided to trust our luck and took a taxi. When we arrived two hours later we were thankful to get the last two rooms in a cheap motel.

Nyale are small, colored sea worms found in tropical waters. When seasonal, marine and lunar conditions converge — usually February or March — they spawn on beaches along Lombok's south coast, especially Seger Beach near Kuta. Eaten raw or grilled with coconut and spices, nyale are considered to be an aphrodisiac. But the festival is much more than a chance to catch a few buckets of libido-enhancing sea worms. It is steeped in myth and traditions close to the heart of Lombok's Sasak people. A beautiful young princess, Mandalika, was being pursued by suitors from rival kingdoms. Finding herself unable to choose among them and fearing her choice would fuel a war, she threw herself off a cliff into the sea at Seger Beach. When people searched for her all they found were the writhing nyale, thought to be the remnants of her long hair. Her transformation became a parable about sacrificing for the greater good and another reminder to avoid confrontation.

We didn't know this when we sat down on the beach under a tree to get respite from the fierce midday heat. As the afternoon progressed more people began to appear. Truckloads of young men dressed in brightly colored outfits and carrying instruments were followed by groups of exquisitely quaffed young women. Amid thumping drums and a cheering crowd, the procession headed down the main road. Sitting high on a platform carried by an entourage of young men was a stunning Mandalika dressed in gold cloth.

That evening we chose a simple warung on the beach for dinner. As we ate Herman chatted with the restaurant owner, Made. A soft-spoken, middle-aged man, Made told us that early the next morning people would gather at Seger Beach to catch nyale, but before that there would be a dramatic re-enactment of the Mandalika legend. If we wanted to see this we would need to be there about 3:00 am. Made had planned to go by boat to catch nyale, but when Herman asked if he'd drive us to the beach he willingly agreed.

Just before 3:00 am Made's van pulled up in front of our motel and we joined the flood of cars and motorcycles heading east. When we arrived at the parking lot our jaws dropped. Before us were several thousand motorcycles. Walking through crowded food stalls we glimpsed the Mandalika drama taking place on a giant stage, but decided to make straight for the beach. In the water were masses of people with all kinds of lights — flashlights, headlamps, cell phones, tablets and other devices. We followed Made with his improvised net and bucket. When he spotted a good-sized worm he'd scoop it up and toss it into the bucket. In the midst of the hubbub, a television crew strode calmly through the water, cameras perched on their shoulders and microphones in hand to capture this magic moment. As the first light of dawn broke over the headland we forgot our tiredness and received a new injection of life. How fortunate we were to have witnessed this spectacle, as we had been in Bali with Galungan. It was as though we had been led to these places at this time. I began to see why many Indonesians believe in a world beyond the rational.

Next day over lunch Bruce complained of stomach cramps, so we returned to our room to rest but by late afternoon the pain had increased. I had seen a clinic sign on the main road so I set out on foot to see if I could find a doctor. When I reached the clinic I learned that the two doctors were away but their assistant kindly offered to fetch Bruce with his motorcycle. As soon as Bruce arrived at the clinic he was given a saline drip in case he was dehydrated. Since the head doctor was due to return later that evening, the staff suggested that Bruce stay overnight at the clinic. When I saw his air-conditioned unit with attached bathroom, refrigerator and satellite television, I had second thoughts about returning to the motel.

The next day Bruce was feeling better so was discharged with medications. Because this was our friends' last day on Lombok, we decided to have a farewell lunch at a restaurant high up on the hillside overlooking Kuta. Halfway through lunch Bruce excused himself. His stomach cramps had returned and he was in severe pain. We said a quick and sad farewell to our friends and went straight back to the clinic. When Dr Dibrata appeared later in the afternoon he tried several tests but wasn't sure what was ailing Bruce. He then phoned a colleague in the regional city of Praya about 20 kilometers away. As soon as he finished the call he said, "Come on. We're going for a ride in the ambulance."

While Bruce lay in the back with the assistant gently massaging his stomach, I rode up front with the doctor-cum-driver. He chatted constantly while driving at breakneck speed and asking questions of his assistant. Now and again a squeaky voice on his mobile phone would interrupt with "Oo ee, oo ah ah, ting tang, walla walla bing bang" — the witchdoctor song I remembered from my childhood. Dibrata would answer with a polite *walaikum*. I couldn't help but laugh at the incongruity of it all. As he drove Dibrata cursed drivers blocking his way and for not heeding the ambulance's flashing light. He pointed out that Indonesians tend not to take much notice of such things. "When they first installed traffic lights in Jakarta," he said, "it took years before motorists obeyed them."

On our arrival at his friend's clinic we were whisked into the surgery. An ultrasound scan of Bruce's stomach and abdomen ruled out gall stones or appendicitis. After a quick confab between the two doctors, Diabrata said nonchalantly, "Stomach gas." That was all? Stomach gas? Well, that, and a bit of constipation. So it was back to Kuta in the ambulance and a second night in the clinic apartment. This time I was invited to stay and served dinner as well. Next morning when we left we felt more like honored guests than patients.

It was time to move on and Made's son, with all the charm and geniality of his father, agreed to be our driver. We made our way up Lombok's east coast and into the interior of the island past fields of rice, tobacco, cashew and mango trees. Mosques were being built or restored in every town we passed through. Lombok's poor cousin label didn't seem to fit. Our destination was the little hamlet of Tetebatu at the foot of the island's highest peak, the majestic 3,726-meter volcano, Mount Rinjani. We checked into a two-story, thatched bungalow and were looking forward to eating at the elevated restaurant with stunning rice-field views recommended in the guide book, but it was closed so we headed into town. After walking up and down we found a little warung with a sign that boasted 'bloody tasty Sasak dishes'. Was this an Australian hangout? We knocked but couldn't find a soul. Just as we were about to leave a man entered from the street.

"I saw you walking down the road and followed you. You want dinner? No problem. Please sit."

We had just met Kuss, the owner, who was expecting another couple, but they never showed so we were an unexpected blessing. The menu looked impressive but after eliminating all the things that weren't available we settled for Kuss's recommendation. Just then the heavens opened in a tropical downpour. Like many Indonesian restaurants this had no solid walls so we sat and listened to the rain pounding on the corrugated iron roof. Kuss joined us as we sipped our drinks. Suddenly he jumped up and pointed beneath my chair.

"Watch out!" he yelled.

Instinctively I retracted my feet. When I looked down I saw a dark brown snake more than a meter long slide from underneath them and cross the floor to a crack in the wall. Kuss called his father who appeared armed with a stick. Despite my protest to let it go, the snake was dead within minutes. It turned out that my safety wasn't the only concern.

"Not a good omen," said Kuss.

Next morning was bright and clear so we were able to get a good view of Rinjani soaring above the rice fields. After breakfast two young men appeared with motorcycles to take us to the Air Jeruk Manis (sweet lemon water) waterfall in Mt

Rinajni National Park. A 30-minute ride over potholed roads brought us to the park entrance, from where we walked a couple of kilometers through the forest to the falls.

"Local people believe the water at these falls makes you younger and prevents baldness," said the older of the two.

"Ah," I thought. "My kind of waterfall!"

We could hear the water before we saw it, crashing 30 meters into a deep pool. As soon as we reached the pool the younger man plunged in and swam to the cascading water. He clambered up the rock face like a gecko skittering across a wall. I followed and with his help joined him on a narrow rock ledge. The water felt so rejuvenating I could understand how it had acquired its name.

Our Australian friends had recommended we visit the Gilis, three small islands off northwest Lombok. Trewangan, the largest, is reputedly 'the party island' popular with a younger crowd. Meno next door is more sedate and appeals to the 'get-away-from-it-all' types. And Air is somewhere between. We spent two days on Meno and three on Air. The perahu we took from Lombok dropped us on Meno's beach at an ecolodge where we took the last available room. Given the price it was a steal, but due to an island-wide electricity failure there was no hot water for bathing. Nevertheless, we had stunning sunset views of Bali's Mount Agung, a candlelight dinner on the beach, and friendly young staff who couldn't do enough to help us. While paradise is nice, it's better with electricity.

Not being avid divers or snorkelers, we chose to explore the island instead. We rubbed shoulders with many people but two stand out. One was Boulong, a taciturn, middle-aged man whose life mission is to save Meno's turtles from extinction. He gathers their eggs and nurtures the young turtles in tanks until they are about eight months, then releases them into the sea. He spends around 100,000 rupiah (US$12) a day on feed, a significant sum for a Meno villager, so seeks donations for his work. We were glad to contribute.

The other person who made a deep impression was Suparto, a teacher at the island school. Dressed in a T-shirt, shorts and baseball cap, he was eager to give us a tour of the facility and tell us about the school. He was one of eight teachers for Meno's 100 primary and pre-primary students, although being from the community was paid only a fraction of the government appointees. But as he showed us through the minimally equipped classrooms, his pride in the school seeped through. Students were taught Sasak, Bahasa Indonesian and English, as well as social studies, mathematics, biology, computer skills and religion. Suparto explained that although there isn't a long break in the school year, there are many holidays to honor Indonesia's multicultural mosaic and national celebrations.

After two nights on Meno we took a boat to Gili Air. With 1,500 inhabitants it is the most populous of the three islands. Like the other two, it has no vehicles. The only transport is by bicycle or horse-drawn cidomo. While fishing and coconuts provide some income, tourism fuels the island's economy. It was the only place we saw a concerted effort to deal with the ubiquitous rubbish that disfigures an otherwise pristine environment, fed in part by plastic water bottles used by foreign tourists.

One afternoon we stopped at a small shop where several women were milling around. One of them demanded to know where we were from. As soon as we said USA, she burst out with a passionate "Obama!" Her delight was understandable, given that the former US president spent several years in Jakarta as a boy. Her enthusiasm led her to shower us with gifts of tapioca wafers, water spinach and coconut salad. We initially declined her kind offer but when she made it clear that was not an option, we gratefully accepted.

Food is pivotal part of any culture but in Indonesia it occupies a special place. Eating at beachfront restaurants on a warm tropical night is hard to match. Our favorite restaurant on Gili Air was Scallywags. With historical décor, piped music, and a good internet connection it was a cut above the rest. Their sumptuous salad bar, seafood kebabs and mouthwatering desserts would have done any restaurant proud. Relaxing after dinner on a beach lounge chair and watching the moon rise above Mount Rinjani made for a near-perfect dining experience. But what really kept us coming back to Scallywags were the engaging young staff, mostly college students who had the service thing down pat and proudly practiced their English with an unfailing smile.

All too soon it was time to return to Lombok and take a plane to Bali before the long flight home. When the little fishing perahu picked us up from the beach we didn't want to leave. That night in Lombok we had dinner with an acquaintance of Herman's who had arranged our accommodation and an all-day excursion to the north of the island. On the way back we stopped at a site where our host was building bungalows by the beach. With typical Indonesian indirectness, he tried to interest us investing in this development. Spending time in this magnificent place among such accommodating people in such a vibrant culture was most compelling. But living half a world away injected hard reality into that scenario. We thanked him for his kind offer and promised to consider it, as well as recommend it to others, *mungkin* and *belum*.

PURA VIDA

. . . . .

Although Costa Rica has much to offer visitors, it was its rain forests that captured me. After a little research I settled on the Osa Peninsula in the southeast of the country, home to the Corcovado National Park. Hailed as one of the world's few remaining pristine rain forests, it boasts hundreds of species of birds and mammals, many endangered. And lots of rain, especially in the rainy season, euphemistically called 'the green season' in the tourist bumf. It rarely stopped raining for the five days I was there. There were short interludes of 'light rain' and odd flashes of 'misting rain', usually followed by torrential rain fed by hurricane activity.

One reason I chose Bahía Paraíso (Paradise Bay) Rain Forest Lodge as my destination was its website description of how to get there from the capital, San José. After a 40-minute flight in a small aircraft to the town of Palmar Sur, I would be whisked away by taxi to the sleepy port of Sierpe, where I would board a boat to take me down the mangrove-lined Sierpe River to the Pacific Ocean and along the coast to my rendezvous with paradise. Delightful.

Palmar Sur's minimum-length airstrip was paved but as narrow as an Irish country lane. As we prepared to land, I noticed another plane taxiing down the runway. Fortunately the pilot noticed it too, and at the last minute sent our plane zooming off in a loop before returning for a second attempt.

Stepping out of the aircraft, I and four other passengers were greeted by a taxi driver and a bevy of young boys determined to carry our luggage ten meters to a waiting van. With his best Spanglish, the driver sorted out the destination of the other two couples but didn't seem to know what to do with me. Having nearly missed the flight in San José because I didn't hear a boarding call, I wondered if I'd taken the correct flight. Then I uttered the name Adrian, the person with whom I'd made my booking in San José.

"Ah, Mr. John!" exclaimed the driver, as if he'd discovered a long-lost friend.

This unsettled me a little but I decided to relax and trust those designated to take care of me, an attitude I found helpful a number of times during my stay in Costa Rica.

Arriving at Sierpe's Restaurante Las Vegas, the driver delivered me into hands of my next chaperone, Rafael. A short, skinny runt of a man, he was introduced as el capitán, a title I would soon discover was thoroughly deserved. He pointed to the dock and a six-meter boat with a 115-horsepower outboard. About half the seating area was covered with a sun canopy that didn't look like it would be put to much use this day. I picked up my case and joined two Austrian girls, a stout middle-aged man of ample girth, a gaunt young man with a red bandanna who surely descended from pirate stock, and a matronly woman cradling a carton of eggs.

Within a short time we pulled away from the dock and wound our way down the muddy river. The rain soon escalated from a fine mist to constant drizzle to heavy sheets. I tried keeping my eyes peeled for Cayman crocodiles but this became futile. Visibility was decreasing by the minute and the boat offered little protection from the driving rain. At one point I tried squatting on my haunches next to the luggage hold, facing the stern to avoid the direct impact of the rain. This had little effect other than cause the pirate to smirk.

As I reconciled myself to a long and wet ride I noticed small waves rolling toward us. Rafael cut the engine and let the boat drift while he distributed life jackets. Apparently, up to this point such devices were of no consequence. 'Now the fun really starts' seemed to be the message. Once everyone had donned their jackets he restarted the engine and headed to the open sea. The closer we came to the mouth of the river the more I wondered how we'd make it through. Rafael knows these waters like the back of his hand, I reminded myself. Trust him.

With one hand on the tiller and an eagle eye on the ever-changing surf, he maneuvered the boat into position and with sudden acceleration drove it toward the open sea, only to back off at the last minute, go around in a large arc, and try again. At the eighth or ninth attempt I was sure he would call it quits. Not Rafael. After cresting a wave the boat would drop into the following trough with a thud that felt like it was about to break into pieces. I imagined myself swimming ashore, although trying to find my way through mangrove swamps, even without the excitement of meeting a Cayman croc, was daunting. None of my fellow travelers seemed panicked, which was reassuring. When we finally made it over the breakers and headed along the coast I relaxed a little. Then I noticed we could no longer see land. Another boat could have been meters away and we'd never have known.

At one point it seemed we had changed direction and were heading toward the vague outline of the coast. "We are here," I silently rejoiced. Then I remembered seeing on the lodge website that Paradise Bay was protected by small islets not visible here. The pirate and the woman with eggs exited the boat in rolling surf. As they waded ashore I thought, "I sure hope whoever eats those eggs appreciates what that woman went through to bring them here!"

Rafael then turned the boat around and headed back to the open sea. I wondered how far it was to Bahía Paraíso. I was soaked to the bone and beginning to shiver. After another 20 minutes of buffeting seas and pouring rain I could just make out two craggy rocks in the distance. Visions of a warm shower and dry clothes pranced around in my head. Rafael steered the boat through the narrow passage between the islets and headed for the beach.

As I glimpsed my first look at 'home' for the next five days, several figures came running down to the shore to meet us, umbrellas in hand. It seemed too little too late, but I appreciated the gesture. First was a strapping young man who introduced himself as Andrés, the manager, and who insisted on carrying my case ashore. He also helped the two young Austrian women and the older man, whom he introduced as his father. His father and I had hardly exchanged a word since meeting several hours ago, but before the week was out I would come to know him in ways I never expected.

As soon as we made it to the thatched-roof restaurant, Andrés offered me the traditional welcoming cocktail. As I stretched out my hand to take the glass he noticed I was shaking.

"Would you like to change your clothes?" he inquired.

"That sounds a wonderful idea!" I replied.

Twenty minutes later I returned to the dining room, having shed my drowned-rat persona and ready for the newcomers' briefing. As I sat down for the first of many exquisitely presented meals at Bahía Paraíso I said a short, silent prayer of thanks. After lunch the resident guide, Freddy Cruz, joined me at my table.

"You've made it through the worst part," he confided. "Going back is easier than coming out."

Glad to know I had earned my stripes, I asked if there had ever been any accidents on the trip.

"As a matter of fact," he said matter-of-factly, "there was one yesterday. A boat overturned but another came to its rescue and no one was harmed. There were eight people on board, including a child. But in the ten months I've been here it was only the second accident and no one has drowned."

Over the next four days I would get to know Freddy more. The youngest of three brothers, he was passionate about two things: improving his English and expanding his knowledge of the rain forest's flora and fauna. If he wasn't serving at the bar — and sometimes when he was — he would hold a plastic-coated sheet from his bird book and mouth the English pronunciation of familiar species. One night after watching *American Beauty* together, I asked Freddy how much he understood. He said he followed much of it but relied mostly on the Spanish subtitles. When I tried this I found the gap between the printed and spoken word so great that I wondered how much of the movie he understood.

* * *

When I booked my 'green season' package it included three tours — one to Corcovado National Park, another to Caño Island about 20 kilometers off the coast, and a canoe trip up the Rio Claro. Because of heavy rainfall and the hurricane-affected weather all seemed unlikely. Nevertheless the staff did their utmost to make my stay worthwhile. The next morning

Freddy suggested we head for the Rio Claro, a 45-minute walk along the coast. Our first stop was the tropical garden surrounding the lodge with its dazzling array of plants. The old name signs were devoid of information but Freddy's encyclopedic knowledge filled in the blanks. Before tackling the plants he made one request of me.

"I always ask guests to correct my English. Most people say they will but they don't. Please do."

I promised I would.

The garden contained plants from around the world in addition to local varieties. We began with citronella. After rubbing it between his fingers, Freddy passed a piece of it to me.

"You know this?" he asked.

I felt like a schoolboy on the first day of term being asked the question that would determine his ranking in class.

"Uh, lemon grass?"

"No, citronella, from Sri Lanka."

"Ah, so it is!" I said, with an I-really-knew-that intonation.

Freddy probably tried this question on every visitor at the start of the tour to establish his place in the scheme of things. I wondered what he did with those who answered correctly. Maybe he saved the Sri Lanka part for them. Regardless, he had me at his mercy and I dutifully followed him from tree to tree, plant to plant. He showed me heliconia, wild ginger, kapok trees, strangle fig trees and beach almonds. The latter were prized by the scarlet macaws that graced the area with their brilliant blue, yellow and vermilion coloring.

Before we had gone far Freddy drew my attention to a tree.

"You know Chanel No. 5?" he inquired.

"I'm familiar with the name," I replied.

"This is the plant they make the perfume from. Here, take it," he gestured, plucking a flower from a branch and thrusting it under my nose. "Nice smell, eh?"

"Wow! That's sensational," I exclaimed.

Mindful of my promise to improve his English, I added, "Scent, rather than smell."

He made a mental note of my pearl of wisdom.

"Have it," he said, "give it to the someone special in your life."

The someone special in your life! The phrase bounced around in my head like an echo in a closed room. Where on earth did he learn that I wondered? Probably not from *American Beauty*. Most guides would have said 'for your wife' or 'for your girlfriend.' Did they have culturally correct guide-training schools in Costa Rica or was Freddy more astute than I'd given him credit for?

The trail followed the coastline closely, merging with secluded coves fed from waterfalls cascading down the hillside. Freddy shared his knowledge of plants and birds, punctuated by periods of silence. Just as I was wondering how far we had to go, our track descended to a sandy beach, on which was a large tent and pathways bordered by pieces of carved driftwood. It seemed like a permanent dwelling, which puzzled me, since Freddy had told me that in Costa Rica all land 50 meters back from the high tide mark is public access and can be used only for temporary structures, which must be moved at least once a month. This looked like it had been here since the 1970s. When I asked Freddy about this, he shrugged his shoulders and smiled.

Ricardo, the tent's permanent temporary resident, emerged from the tent and greeted us. His retiring manner and unforced smile suggested someone who took each day as it came. His striped swimming trunks looked like his primary, maybe only, set of clothes. Perhaps he had a T-shirt with 'Save the Rainforest' scrawled across the back when cruise ships visited during the dry season. Freddy informed me that Ricardo made most of his modest annual income from these invasions of foreigners, whom he took upriver by canoe to explore the tropical jungle.

However he wasn't going to make much off me this day. The night before, torrential rain had caused the raging waters of the Rio Claro to burst through the sandbar at the river's mouth. The Rio Claro was now anything but claro. Without getting soaked and risk being swept out to sea there was no way we could reach the canoes, let alone travel upstream against the surging current. So much for the lodge's website promo: 'You will be able to swim in sweet water and then slowly and safely float into the salt-water reception of the ocean.'

But my disappointment with the Rio Claro didn't dampen my enthusiasm. I still had three more days and two other excursions to look forward to — Corcovado National Park and Caño Island. Each morning I would check with Andrés about the likelihood of these happening. He'd radio Rafael in Sierpe but his responses were not encouraging. Short lulls between persistent squalls and driving wind ruled out both destinations. Most days Caño Island was not visible from the mainland. When occasionally it was, it reared up from the sea like the giant monolith Uluru in central Australia.

To compensate for missing the national park, Andrés suggested an alternative. Adjacent to Bahía Paraíso was a 500-hectare biological reserve attached to another lodge. Andrés assured me it contained the same bio-diversity as the famous Corcovado National Park and said that the owners had given permission to take guided tours through the reserve. Verena, one of the two young Austrian guests, wanted to come too, so we formed a threesome. Foursome actually, because Rocco, the lodge's resident mutt, decided to join us. Freddy said Rocco always followed the tourists but never the staff. No doubt he relished the attention visitors paid him; perhaps in return he saw it as his duty to protect them from danger.

We took off up the hill behind the lodge to a lookout with a 180-degree view of Drake Bay. From the lookout we trekked along the escarpment before coming to the trailhead into the forest. Every now and again Freddy would stop, point, and with unrestrained glee proclaim, "See!" On closer inspection and usually with the help of binoculars we would notice a red-capped manikin, a rufous-tailed jacama or spider monkeys. The prize was a brownish-gray blur high up in a tree that turned out to be a sloth, as languid as its name implies. I couldn't resist sharing this gem with Freddy, who dutifully added 'slothful' to his collection of rare and precious English words.

A short way into the walk Freddy pointed to fresh footprints.

"Deer," he said authoritatively.

But about a kilometer further on he stopped again, got down on his haunches, and more thoroughly examined the prints. A slight frown came over his face.

"Perhaps it is wild pig, peccary."

I had read that peccaries could be the most dangerous animals in the rain forest, especially if surprised or threatened. They are known to take on jaguars and pumas and emerge victorious. I looked at Verena, who was looking at Freddy. Just as I was about to open my mouth she beat me to it.

"What should we do if we meet the pig?"

Bang on, I thought.

"Climb a tree, quickly," replied Freddy.

I looked around for likely trees. All I could see were straight up and down and as slippery in the falling rain as a greased pole. Sensing our anxiety, Freddy jumped into the breach.

"Don't worry," he said. "You rarely see peccaries here. I've never come across one."

With these reassuring words we kept walking deeper into the forest, but more cautiously. Freddy spent less time looking up into trees and more time down at the ground. After a couple of hundred meters we came across a mound of freshly upturned earth.

"Termite nest," said Freddy.

What he didn't say was patently clear to all of us. That pig was not far off. At that moment I noticed that Rocco was no longer with us. He would disappear from time to time but return shortly after. Suddenly I felt vulnerable. Trust Freddy, I kept reminding myself. He knows this place, he knows these creatures. We kept walking but closer together than before. Then in the midst of the gentle pitter-patter of rain splashing on leaves and the squelch of our boots in the mud a sharp snapping sound rang out. Freddy froze. Verena and I exchanged nervous glances.

"Run!" yelled Freddy.

Just then Rocco's bark echoed through the forest. My adrenalin was pumping full bore. We found a few trees that angled slightly but getting a firm grip on their slimy trunks was near impossible. Freddy helped Verena hoist herself up a tree on one side of the trail before finding one for himself a few meters away. I seized on one opposite Verena but was only a meter or so off the ground so looked for other options. An old-growth tree with hanging vines nearby looked promising. Would I have time to change trees before the pig appeared? Could I make it up to a higher foothold? And what about Andrés' warning never to put your hands on trees and plants in the rain forest? Casting caution aside, I jumped to the ground, raced to the other tree, and hauled myself up using the vines like a rope.

As I did Verena called out, "I don't know how much longer I can hold on."

"Why don't you join me?" I suggested, since there seemed to be enough space below me to get her safely off the ground.

She fled her tree and clawed her way up mine. I tried to help but her tight jeans made it difficult for her to stretch her legs and grip the trunk. I barely had the strength to hold on to the vines with one hand and pull her up with the other. We held our breath, wondering what the pig was up to. Then the silence was shattered by Rocco's bark. Had he cornered the pig? Was the pig about to attack him? What if Rocco should be injured or die? For a moment I was more concerned about his fate than ours; the two seemed so intertwined.

After about ten minutes Freddy decided to scope out the situation and returned shortly afterwards, beckoning us down. Since our only option was to go back the way we'd come, this meant walking through the area where we had first heard the pig. Freddy informed us that the snapping sound was the noise peccaries make when ready to attack. I was not sure I wanted to know this at that moment. We retraced our steps, Freddy in front, Verena in the middle, and I in the rear. About every 30 seconds I turned around to check we were not being followed by an angry pig.

Just as we were beginning to relax our guard there was a shuffle in the bushes. We froze. I looked around for suitable trees to climb but there were none. Then Rocco bounded out of the bushes and greeted us waving his tail. You could hear a collective sigh of relief. A little further on we stumbled upon a cross made of sapling branches tied together with rusted wire. I wondered what it commemorated.

Before our departure the next morning we were treated to a full Tico (Costa Rican) breakfast of cereal, scrambled eggs, rice, beans, fried plantains, fruit, toast, coffee and endless glasses of pureed frescas. I was reluctant to eat much before the journey but the staff had put so much effort into this final grand repast it felt insulting to refuse it. I was barely half way through the meal when the boat arrived, so I was able to politely excuse myself. It was then I learned that I wasn't the only passenger that day. Andrés' mother, father and 84-year-old grandmother were to accompany me.

Andrés told me that before making this trip his grandmother had never seen the ocean. In this tiny Central American country she had never ventured outside her local area. Her first experience of the ocean was coming down the Sierpe River and along the coast in a flimsy boat at this time of year. What's more, she had traveled on the day another boat had capsized so had been privy to the accident. I wondered what she was thinking as we walked down to the beach. In the falling rain Andrés picked up his grandmother like a parent would a child, walked through the waves, and gently lowered her into the boat. His mother and father came next then I followed. This time I wore swimming trunks, T-shirt and rain poncho.

About half way along the coast we pulled into another lodge. Andrés had told me that if a certain bridge was not under water, I would take a taxi from here to Drake Bay airport and fly back to San José. As we nosed into the dock Rafael was talking to Andrés on his mobile phone. He then addressed me in a flurry of Spanish, followed by Andrés' father and mother, all vainly trying to make me understand. In desperation, Andrés' mother thrust forward her two hands, pretending to hold the steering wheel of a car. Ah, I thought, I'm going by taxi after all. Just to be sure I asked to speak with Andrés.

"Hi John," said Andrés. "Another slight change of plans. You can't get through by taxi so you have two choices. You can come back to the lodge and spend another night here and fly back tomorrow, or you can go with my parents by car back to San José today. Which would you prefer?"

Apart from having booked a bus tour the following day, the idea of flying back to San José wasn't appealing. There was so much cloud on the trip down I'd hardly seen anything, so I told Andrés I'd be glad to travel with his parents. Turning to his mother, I repeated her car driving histrionics. She beamed the broadest of smiles. It was like, 'Houston, we have contact.'

After the boat pulled out from the lodge's dock, the rain tapered off to a light drizzle for the rest of the journey. Once ashore, we changed clothes and headed to the Restaurante Las Vegas. How I ended up with fried chicken when I thought I'd ordered a chicken sandwich, I'm not sure. Perhaps the Mexico-Costa Rica soccer game blasting overhead had something to do with it. Once we had downed our food and drinks we packed into a compact Toyota and were on our way. Father drove, mother sat in the front passenger seat, while I hunkered down in the back with grandma. She was like a little bird that occasionally chirped a word or two but mostly remained silent. Apart from helping her adjust her seatbelt or open her purse, I tried not to inflict my low level of conversational Spanish on her.

Having visited Mexico and Guatemala, I knew Latin Americans had a different relationship to driving than those of us from more staid cultures. I'd experienced their grab-the-initiative-and-keep-it-at-all-costs mode of driving, but I wasn't prepared for Andrés' father's wild rampage. He seemed intent on trying to break the world speed record for four-door sedans on two-lane roads under hurricane-affected weather conditions. When he took his first 90-degree corner at 100 kilometers an hour I thought he was just showing off. But when he continued to perform such gymnastic feats I began to doubt our prospects of making it back alive. His favorite tactic was to try to pass a long line of vehicles, including at least one mammoth Del Monte truck, while heading into a blind corner. Rapid acceleration and deceleration seemed to be key. Every now and again his wife would squawk in protest but her husband ignored her and surged ahead.

My immersion into the world of Tico driving would not have been quite so unnerving if it hadn't been for the massive landslides caused by recent heavy rains. Entire hillsides had been dislodged and were strewn across the road. We would tear around corners to be confronted by earth-moving equipment trying to remove piles of dirt and trees blocking the road. I prayed we had good brakes. After several close encounters I wondered if Andrés' father might be a little more cautious, but they only egged him on. These were challenges any self-respecting Tico driver was meant to overcome.

Such feats called for constant refueling, and not just of the vehicle. Forty minutes after leaving Restaurante Las Vegas we stopped at a roadside café. Andrés' father stormed into the shop and came back laden with snacks and bottled water. Two hours later we pulled into a roadside diner. When I politely passed on the beef stew with bean and eggs combo the others looked at me in amazement. I settled for a mug of hot chocolate and turned my attention to the latest developments in the Mexico-Costa Rica game. Stomachs dragging on the ground, we returned to the car and the home stretch.

When this day started I thought my boat journey or rain forest walk would be the things I'd remember most from my time in the Osa Peninsula. But the car ride surpassed both. As we came closer to San José I discovered that Andrés' family didn't actually live in San José but in the ancient capital of Cartago 20 kilometers east. I thought I would take a bus from there to San José and a taxi from the bus station to the home of my friend Sandy. When we arrived at the family home I called Sandy to get her advice.

"OK," she said cautiously. "But be very careful when you get to the San José bus station. Don't take your eyes off your luggage for a second and make straight for the taxis."

Andrés' father's offer to drive me to the Cartago bus station gave me one more chance to sample his exquisite driving skills. The fact that we were driving through built-up suburbs didn't deter him. Entire blocks flashed past in a blur. Traffic lights and stop signs seemed like unnecessary decor.

Within minutes we were at the bus station. As I was about to thank him for this day-of-a-lifetime he said something about a taxi collectivo and trotted over to a group of taxi drivers huddled on the sidewalk. When he returned a few minutes later he tried to explain something to me. My grasp of Spanish took a quantum leap but it seemed that I had a choice between waiting for more passengers and getting a cheaper rate, or going alone and paying more. Given the events of the day and my desire to return to the comfort and security of Sandy's home, I chose the latter. With a handshake that seemed to never end, Andrés' father looked me in the eyes and said a hearty *mucho gusto*. All I could muster in response was a feeble *muchas gracias*.

Next morning I went on an all-day tour of a volcano, butterfly farm, waterfall and river cruise. But from the luxury of a tourist coach and with the day scripted to the minute, this felt tame compared to my recent experiences. While other passengers talked about hot springs and canopy tours, I could only think of the people who had welcomed me into their world and shared their lives so generously with me — Rafael and Ricardo, Freddy and Andrés, the two Austrians, Andrés' father and mother, grandmother and more.

As our tour progressed, Jorge, our guide, managed to take a crowd of reticent foreigners and forge us into a group. One way he did this was teaching a little tiquismos or Costa Rican Spanish. The most memorable phrase was *pura vida*, which I'd heard everywhere from the travel agency booking clerk to the barman at Bahía Paraíso. Literally, it means 'pure life' but colloquially it's more akin to 'great' or 'terrific.' Before our first stop of the day Jorge had all of us responding in unison to his questions with a vibrant *pura vida*. Something about the way it rolls off your tongue makes it sound just right. I couldn't think of a more appropriate phrase to sum up my time in Costa Rica. *Pura vida!*

AMBASSADORS
AT LARGE

. . . . .

It had been a productive week planning for the future of this
remote Aboriginal community but everyone seemed ready to
wrap it up. In his closing remarks the Institute's director praised
the progress the people had made since they quit the nearby town
and resettled on tribal land. Then quite unexpectedly he asked,
"Wouldn't it be something if this community was represented
at the launch of the first African Human Development Project
in Kenya?" Silence reigned over the gathering. The community
had sent members to programs in other parts of Australia, but
Africa? Few, if any, Aboriginal Australians had been to Africa in
1975. Who would represent the community and who from our
staff would accompany them?

There was so much to do to following the planning
consultation that the idea of sending a delegation to Africa

took a back seat. It did seem a bit far-fetched, although the Institute was known for its audacious acts and symbolic gestures. Then one morning at the monthly council meeting the question came up for discussion. Names were put forward but the most likely candidates had been on trips. The elders said they would talk it over among themselves and with the community and decide at the next meeting.

After that meeting, I ran into one of my colleagues returning to our staff residence.

"So what happened about the Africa trip?" I asked.

"You'll never believe who the council chose."

"Doesn't sound like I would," I replied.

"Stan and Rose," he said with a grin.

Stan was the council chairman, so it didn't surprise me that his name had been put forward, quite possibly by him. But it wasn't local politics that concerned me. It was the fact that Stan, like many middle-aged men in the community, had a weakness for alcohol and could easily succumb to it. Younger than Stan, Rose was less prone to drinking and had impressed since becoming the clinic assistant. When she hit town, however, she often fell prey to drink and suffered the ensuing violence and abuse.

But the council had chosen and our staff were reluctant to intervene. We needed to decide who among us would accompany Stan and Rose. Time was short and preparations needed to be made. At our weekly staff meeting I sat up with a jolt when our director suggested I go. I had not left the community for some time so I welcomed a break, but Africa was a daunting prospect, especially since we only had a month to prepare.

I immediately started compiling a list of things to do in order to make it to Kenya on time. Stan and Rose had never owned passports, so that process needed to be set in motion right away. We would all need shots and tickets had to be booked. Our Sydney office normally handled air fares but given the dire straits of our finances at the time they said we would have to cover them, at least for now. The whole undertaking rapidly began to lose its appeal, but I told myself that somehow it would work out.

My first thought was to contact my colleague, Ray, more than 3,000 kilometers away in Perth, raising money and in-kind support for the project. He had a reputation for pulling off the impossible so I phoned him on my next visit to town and explained the situation. Did he think he could convince Qantas to donate two tickets to Africa within a couple of weeks? And could he please begin the passport application process for Stan and Rose?

"I'll see what I can do," he said. "By the way, what about your ticket?"

"I was told I need to come up with the money for that and they'll reimburse me later. My pickings are slim but I have a couple of ideas. You focus on our two friends for now."

A week later Ray telegrammed to say he had phoned a member of the federal parliament, who had called the CEO of Qantas and received a favorable reply. Tickets would be on their way, along with passport application forms. He suggested the three of us come down to Perth a few days ahead of our departure and he would find a way to outfit Stan and Rose with travel essentials. What a week ago seemed almost impossible, now felt more doable.

But I still had serious misgivings about the whole venture. Stan and Rose had never flown on a plane larger than a single-engine Cessna on the 20-minute flight from town. How would they handle being confined in an aircraft for long periods of time? How would they would deal with immigration and other authorities? What might they do once they encountered a large city, even one as modest as Perth? The only towns they had experienced had populations of a few hundred. I tried to prepare them for what they would encounter but it seemed futile. Their world was so limited compared to the one they were about to enter.

* * *

On the day we left home a large crowd gathered at the river to see us off. The two-hour trip down river and across the gulf was the first of many legs on our long journey. Before leaving I sent a message to a friend in town to ask her to meet our boat, then drive us straight to the hospital to get our injections and from there to the airline office. I wanted to avoid any temptations the town offered, beginning with the pub across the road from the boat landing. If Stan and Rose were waylaid there we might never make it out of town, let alone to Africa.

I breathed a sigh of relief as the shuttle van appeared on time at the airline office and we were safely on board. The 100-kilometer drive to the airport passed quickly, despite the oppressive heat. Arriving in Perth five hours later to temperatures half those we had left was the first of many shocks we would experience. Fortunately Ray met us, so we bundled into his Toyota, wrapped ourselves in blankets, and headed to our staff residence. The next couple of days were filled with visits to the passport office, our member of the state parliament, and a downtown department store, where Ray persuaded the manager to outfit our two ambassadors with clothes and shoes at no cost.

Meanwhile, I had to come up with $800 in 48 hours for my ticket. The only person I could think of who had the resources and might be willing to part with them was a former high school teacher. He had taken a strong interest in me as a student and had tried to convince me to study foreign languages so I could enter Australia's diplomatic corps. Instead

I had joined a nondescript, American-based organization that didn't pay salaries and worked with the disenfranchised around the world.

I nervously picked up the phone and dialed his number. We had not spoken since I'd left high school nine years before so his surprise in hearing my voice was not unexpected. He asked me what I was doing and I explained my predicament.

"You call me out of the blue with some story about going to Kenya with two Aborigines and want me to part with 800 smackers?"

"It would only be a loan. I'd pay it back within six months. Be glad to put that in writing if you'd like."

I wasn't sure how to take his laughter at my suggestion. I held my breath and waited for him to respond.

"No doubt about you Sonny Jim. I wouldn't have credited you with such audacity. When do you need the money?"

"Er, tomorrow, actually," I said hesitatingly.

"Tomorrow? Good grief. You don't want much, do you?"

While he hadn't said yes, he hadn't said no either. We chatted and agreed to meet the following day at his local pub. Meeting him face to face seemed to clear the air. After several beers I was relieved when he handed over an envelope and had me sign a note that I would repay the debt.

Next morning I almost cut myself shaving as I listened to the news. Aircraft refuelers at Perth airport were going on strike over a pay increase and all international flights out of Perth were canceled. I called Qantas numerous times but the line was busy. When I finally spoke to someone I was told that instead of going to Mauritius then Nairobi, we would be rerouted via Darwin and Singapore, three times as long and involving two changes of aircraft.

My heart sank. The stress of this convoluted route on my two Aboriginal companions could be disastrous. I wasn't sure how to break the news to them. When I did they didn't seem overly perturbed, probably due their limited knowledge of geography and my failure to mention the time and distances involved. Ironically, we would now go back the way we had just come, and further, in order to fly out of Australia. To lighten the mood Ray proposed we go out to a local restaurant for a good feed. Little did I realize then how astute a suggestion this was.

* * *

The airline caterers had also gone on strike in sympathy with the refuelers, so no meals were served between Perth and Singapore. Stan and Rose kept asking when they'd be getting 'tucker' and I assured them it was on its way, while requesting extra peanuts to fill the void. Stan dealt with the lack of food by ordering more beer. My anxiety level rose with each can he drank. From the look on her face the stewardess shared my concern, but her reluctance to refuse Stan matched my reluctance to play big brother.

The eight-hour flight from Singapore to Mauritius dragged on but with meal service and a couple of movies the trip became less tortuous. Just before arriving the captain announced we would be taken to a hotel for a five-hour layover before resuming our journey to Nairobi. The thought of another ten hours before reaching Kenya sent me into a tailspin but being able to break our journey, breathe fresh air, and have another meal made it more bearable. When the hotel turned out to be on a beach, our mood lightened considerably. It was the best thing to happen since leaving home a week before.

On arrival in Nairobi we were herded into the Department of Health offices for cholera shots that Australian authorities had failed to give us. We sailed through customs, since both Stan and Rose only had carry-on luggage and I a small suitcase. When we came to immigration I went through first then stood and watched the Kenyan officer eye Stan and Rose suspiciously as if to say, "But I thought Australians were mzungus (Europeans)." He'd probably never met an Aboriginal Australian. But it wasn't just the Kenyan who experienced a paradigm shift. Stan and Rose scanned the terminal with a look of wonder on their faces. For the first time outside their community, they were in the majority and blended right in.

As we exited the terminal I was relieved to see a sign with our organization's name on it. Since we were a day late I was concerned we might have to find our own way to the project site. As we traveled across the city, Stan and Rose stared wide-eyed as the drama unfolded before them — buxom women carrying overweight baskets on their heads, highly decorated matutus oozing with passengers, cyclists ringing their bells as they passed within centimeters of our van. And hardly a pale-skinned person anywhere.

Kawangware, the project site, was a slum of about 10,000 inhabitants. Our staff, who had worked for months with community residents to organize the planning consultation, had been given the upstairs floor of a building near the center of the community for their residence and office. It was barely big enough for the regular staff but with an influx of visitors from around the world it was a very tight squeeze. Downstairs a bar pulsated with African dance music around the clock. I became well acquainted with it over the next five days, along with a number of other similar establishments in the neighborhood, as I tried to locate Stan and Rose and woo them back to the consultation. But phrases like 'representing Australia' or 'sharing what you've done' didn't wash. They showed little interest in the proceedings and I began to wonder why we'd come.

When the consultation ended we still had a week before returning to Australia. Most of our staff moved to a different location to write the planning document, so I persuaded Stan and Rose to join me and a Kenyan colleague in visiting some of Nairobi's historic landmarks. But they had little desire to play tourist. Kenya's struggle to throw off the yoke of colonialism and forge a modern nation out of competing tribes didn't interest them. During the evenings I left them to their own devices, while I joined my colleagues to help with the documentation.

On the second evening just as we were wrapping up for the day, shouting erupted from the entrance to the building. We all looked at one another, puzzled. At that moment our director strode into the room and bellowed "BURBIDGE, come here!" My heart raced as I stood up and followed him out of the room. Then I noticed Stan and Rose staggering down the hallway. As soon as they saw me they let forth a tirade of expletives, most directed at me, some at my colleagues, and a few at white races in general. Fueled with liquid courage, they vented their spleen for all to hear. Two hundred years of repression, suffering and mistreatment of Aboriginal people found a voice in these two drunken souls and I was an easy target for their vitriol. My attempts to intervene only caused them to up the ante. Fortunately, a female colleague who had met Rose in Australia managed to talk her down, while several of my male colleagues attempted the same with Stan.

As I tried to sleep that night I pondered what we were doing to these people, albeit in the name of 'human development'. I couldn't wait for this nightmare to end. The following morning over breakfast one of my colleagues came up to me and explained that a car and driver would be coming to collect Stan and Rose and me and take us on a three-day trip around Kenya. It seemed too good to be true, but I didn't dare question it.

When Stan and Rose appeared they looked the worse for wear. If they had any recollection of the previous evening they didn't let on. As they silently ate their porridge I shared the news of our pending adventure. Rose asked where we'd be going but Stan accepted it with a 'whatever' look. For the next several days we visited a game park, a coffee plantation, a large farm, and several villages in Kenya. Once outside Nairobi Stan and Rose began to shed their withdrawn personas and open up. I took a back seat — literally and figuratively — as our driver, Joseph, peppered them with questions about Australia and told them about life in his village near the town of Machakos.

"Would you like to visit my village?" he asked.

Stan looked at Rose, then at me, before replying.

"Sure," he said.

He didn't appear overly enthusiastic but it was the first time on the trip I'd heard Stan take the initiative. Maybe it was the first time he'd been asked his opinion.

We headed to Joseph's village, which was several kilometers down a dirt track off the main road. As we drove along we passed a primary school with children in the playground.

"That was where I went to school until 12th standard, then I had to work in the fields to help my family," said Joseph. "We are a poor family, with eight children. I used to walk to school and back every day. When I was older I would run. I like running. Do you like running?"

Stan admitted it wasn't his cup of tea. Rose said she once won a race in an interschool sports competition.

We drove on until Joseph pulled up in front of a small shack.

"Welcome to my home," he said proudly.

The look of surprise on Stan and Rose's faces said it all. This simple structure was hardly a step up from the wattle-and-daub houses of their own community.

Joseph's mother greeted us warmly and offered us tea and snacks. As she served us she asked Stan and Rose about their village in Australia. Stan said he was chairman of the council and Rose told of her work in the clinic. Bit by bit they painted a picture of life in their remote community. Afterwards Joseph showed us around his family's farm before we resumed our journey. It felt like the dots were beginning to connect.

Two days later we drove back to Nairobi and headed to the airport to catch our flight to Bombay for a short stop in India, where our staff were preparing to launch their pilot village project. It was my first trip to India so I was apprehensive. Kenya had been a challenge but how would Stan and Rose cope with India's teeming population and cultural diversity?

On arrival at Bombay airport we were met by Hari, the director of our local office, who whisked us away to the staff residence. I was relieved to see that this residence was above a church and not a bar. I mentioned to Hari the problem we'd had with bars in Kawangware and inquired if there were any in the vicinity. He smiled as if he'd been forewarned.

"There are some," he said, "but I will take you to nicer places where we can eat and have a beer. But stay away from that country hooch. Nasty stuff."

The next two days we became acquainted with this fabled city, from Chowpatty Beach to the Gateway of India. Our budget was limited but I needn't have worried since India's generous hospitality prevailed once again. Drinks, snacks, meals, taxis and all other expenses were taken care of. As we explored this labyrinthine city I received lots of stares and requests for money. My two Aboriginal companions were paid no such attention; they melted into the crowd and seemed to relish it.

That evening over dinner Hari told us he had arranged a trip the next day to the village of Maliwada near the city of Aurangabad, 320 kilometers east of Bombay. It was close to the 14th century Daulatabad Fort, once the seat of the Mughal Empire and near the famous Ajanta and Ellora caves. It seemed too good to pass up.

The overnight bus ride to Aurangabad tested our patience and endurance but Hari's wife packed us a substantial hamper and a couple of stops along the way helped break the journey. On reaching Maliwada we were besieged by inquisitive young boys wanting to know where we were from. When I said Australia their eyes lit up at the sound of this famous cricketing country. But curiosity got the better of them.

"But sahib, where are these other people from?" one of them asked, pointing to Stan and Rose.

"They are from Australia too," I explained. "They are Aboriginal Australians, adivasis, tribal people."

At this Stan broke in. "I'm Wunambul mob," he said. "Rosie's Worora."

The young boy took a moment to make sense of this, then turned to Stan.

"I thought you might be from South India," he said. "I know a man from south and he looks just like you."

As we continued our conversation I caught the eye of the chai wallah and held up three fingers. We were enjoying a cup of tea when the tall, lean figure of one my Indian colleagues approached. Word had reached him that we had arrived so we soon found ourselves joining our staff over a tasty lunch of rice and dal.

The rest of the day we visited the village and chatted to people, before climbing the endless stone steps of the nearby fort. For all its historic importance and architectural majesty the fort didn't capture Stan and Rose's imaginations nearly as much as their conversations with villagers. I lost count of the number of times we were welcomed into people's homes and offered chai and biscuits. It made me rethink the value of our Indian Ocean trek.

* * *

Our eight-hour flight to Darwin went quickly compared to other legs of our journey. We had become accustomed to flight routines and a short stop in Singapore helped break the journey. I telegrammed our Darwin staff to advise them of our arrival.

They were keen to hear about our time in Kenya and India, so we arranged a debriefing session later that day. The three of us were jet-lagged so decided to take a nap after breakfast and reconvene in the afternoon. Ten minutes before the session was scheduled to start I knocked on Stan's door, but didn't get a response. I knocked again, louder, but still nothing. I opened the door and found the room empty. I then knocked and entered Rose's room. It, too, was empty, with an open window.

I went straight to the meeting room where Greg, the director, and his wife were waiting along with others.

"They've done a runner," I said. "I don't know where and I don't know Darwin but we've got to find them. We have an early morning flight tomorrow that we have to be on. We'll need to check all the local pubs. Care to help?"

"Sure," said Greg.

This was the part of my assignment I dreaded the most — having to play chaperone, with all the paternalistic overtones that went along with it. We checked out the bars of two nearby hotels but didn't find them. Not all pubs would have been welcoming to Aboriginal patrons, regardless of the law. It was possible they had to go farther afield to find a suitable place.

At our third attempt we lucked out. As I entered the bar I could see Stan and Rose surrounded by a group of men at the far corner of the room. Greg and I approached the group.

"Hi Stan," I said. He looked up and grimaced when he saw me.

I introduced myself to his drinking mates and explained my connection with Stan and Rose. They weren't overly impressed but one of them invited us to join them.

"Thanks, mate, but we have to be going because we've got a meeting we all need to be at."

"Come on," said Stan. "Just one. It won't kill you."

I hesitated and looked at Greg, who shrugged his shoulders.

"OK, just one. But then we need to be on our way."

Twenty minutes later I broke into the conversation.

"Time to go, I'm afraid."

Rose, who had had more than her fair share of drinks, spoke up.

"What's this fucking meeting we have to go to? You gadia are always having meetings. Who says we have to go to your bloody meetings?"

"But Rose, people want to hear about your trip to Africa and India," I pleaded. "They've been waiting more than hour already."

"You can tell 'em all about it. You were there. You don't need us to do that."

Sensing the initiative was fast slipping away from me, Greg interrupted.

"Rose, John can tell his version of what happened but our staff want to hear from you and Stan as well. After all you're probably the first Aboriginal people ever to go to these countries."

"Yeah, we're bloody famous now. Everyone wants to buy us drinks. Everyone except you."

By this time the entire bar had focused its attention on us. I wanted to be anywhere but there at that moment. Greg and I couldn't physically remove Stan and Rose from the premises but more than gentle persuasion was needed.

"Tell you what," I said. "Let's all go now and when the meeting's over we can come back and join your friends."

Lying was never my strong suit but it was all I could think of on the spur of the moment. I put my hand gently on

Stan's shoulder as if to seal the deal. Reluctantly, he stood up and said goodbye to his drinking mates. Rose needed more encouragement but I let Greg handle her. We ambled towards the door and eventually made it to the car.

After our reporting session I telegrammed my colleagues at home, and insisted they have a plane waiting for us at the town airport the next day, so there would be no opportunity to linger before flying back to the community. I didn't want to have to endure another search-and-rescue mission.

* * *

When the van dropped us at the local airport the following morning the pilot had already begun loading the plane. I kept a watchful eye on Stan and Rose in case they decided to make themselves scarce. The airport was a few kilometers from town, and there were no taxis, so they would have had quite a walk if they headed that way.

When the pilot saw us he came over and confirmed that we were the three passengers. I hadn't seen Gary in a while since he'd been in Melbourne for the last six months flying larger aircraft. He'd only recently returned and this was his first flight to the community. We helped him load the plane, since there was a lot of cargo. Apart from mail and store goods there were boxes of medical supplies, staff groceries and our luggage. I was sure we were over the weight limit.

Shortly Gary signaled he was ready to go. He ushered Stan and Rose into the rear seats and indicated to me to join him up front. Within minutes the engine roared and we taxied to the end of the runway. After a few minutes he let out the throttle and we sped down the tarmac and into the air for the last leg of our journey.

We were soon over the tiny town and crossing the muddy waters of the gulf. The sky was crystal clear and the horizon a distant haze. I thought back over the last month and tried to make sense of it all. We had covered nearly 30,000 kilometers, visited four countries, and made connections across cultures that probably had never been made before. It had not been easy for Stan or Rose and it had pushed me to my limits. In fifteen minutes it would be over.

The community airstrip had been carved out of scrub in the mission days. It was minimum length so could only handle small aircraft. At one end was rusted old farm machinery and the other was close to the 'jump-up' at the edge of a vast rocky plateau. In order to not hit the machinery, it was necessary to come in low over the jump-up and make a sharp descent.

As we descended I noticed a tractor and trailer being driven towards the airstrip, loaded with people and many running alongside. Rose let out a loud "Ali!" while Stan grinned sheepishly.

Gary put the plane into a sharp left turn and headed towards the airstrip. We lost altitude quickly and were soon over the end of the runway but the wheels remained stationary. Within seconds the plane was half way down the runway and still hadn't touched ground. Gary pulled back the joystick and the plane rose swiftly. I glanced over and saw sweat pouring down his face.

He then took the plane into a wide arc to gain altitude and did a couple of passes over the tiny settlement. The crowd waved their hands and roared their approval, as if this was all for their entertainment. When we began our descent again, I took a deep breath and felt my body tense. This time the wheels hit the ground about a quarter of the way down the strip. Gary gave it everything he had to bring the plane to a halt, with just meters to spare.

Cheers erupted as we stepped down from the plane and hordes of children raced to embrace Stan and Rose. A colleague waved at me from the back of the crowd. Since I'd joined the organization four years before I'd had some tough assignments, but this took the prize. I felt like resigning but would later come to see that this was just preparing me for greater challenges. I was 26 years old.

DANCING
ON THE DUNES

· · · · ·

Do not take this trip…
- if you prefer things to go according to plan
- if you don't like sand in your food, hair and underwear
- if you object to going unwashed for days on end
- if you're overly sensitive to heat and sun or local food
- if you're not prepared to dig jeeps out of sand, or perhaps wait until dawn to do so
- if being thrown around in the back of a moving vehicle is not your idea of fun
- if you'll be upset when, after three days in the desert, you get back to your oasis hotel to find there's no water in the bathroom…

This was the disclaimer that trip organizer, Martin Gilbraith, offered those contemplating the five-day excursion in Egypt's Western Desert following the Institute's

1996 international conference in Cairo. It was enough to turn away most conferees in favor of trips down the Nile or snorkeling in the Red Sea, but for 20 adventurous souls — young and old, men and women from 10 countries — it was just the turn-on we needed.

Were we disappointed? No way. Not only was the disclaimer fulfilled in detail, it was surpassed on several fronts. But the lure of the desert's ever-changing landscapes, the warm and generous welcome of its inhabitants, and the unputdownable spirit of our Egyptian guides made the disclaimer fade into insignificance.

Before we headed out of Cairo in two minibuses we picked up our last but possibly most important passenger, Reda Abdel Rasoul.

"I am Reda, zee Desert Fox," exclaimed this vibrant young Egyptian with the most engaging smile and thick black mustache. His exuberance masked the fact that he'd been in Cairo to visit his seriously ill brother and had only just decided to make the trip.

Reda was the local organizer of our desert safari. His slick, photographic business card described him as a 'history' teacher but like a number of other educators in desert oases he turned to tour guiding to supplement his meager income. He lived in Bawiti, the largest town in the Bahariya Oasis with a population of 18,000.

Having a history teacher as our guide was an unexpected and valuable bonus. Egypt's ancient roots as a land of pharaohs, pyramids and the fertile Nile Valley is well documented but the Western Desert that occupies much of the country is less well known. Its harsh terrain is not conducive to human settlement but people have managed to eke out a living there for eons. It's a place where myth and history have intertwined, such as the puzzling disappearance of the 50,000-man Persian army under Cambyses II, son of Cyrus the Great, in a sandstorm in the 6th century BC. No trace of this massive force has ever been found.

Throughout the 365-kilometer journey to Bahariya our minds were on more immediate things, as Reda patiently answered our endless questions. Why don't those telegraph poles have wires connecting them? Why are there railway stations in what appears to be nowhere in particular? Where do all those vehicle tracks into the desert lead? What is the Arabic word for...? And more frequently as the hours progressed, how far is it to the nearest rest stop?

The answer to the latter was simple. There is only one stop between Cairo and Bahariya, almost half way. As we entered the large refreshment room we were greeted with ecstatic cries of "Martin! Martin!" Recognizing our British expat leader from many previous trips, the operators of this lonely outpost were effusive in their welcome. Clearly we were in friendly territory. The cold drinks and snacks were delightful, the chance to stretch our legs most welcome, and the toilets were, well...better left to themselves.

Our first clue we were approaching landfall in this endless sea of sand and rock was the police checkpoint near the mining town of Managum, site of Egypt's main source of iron ore, which is transported to Cairo by rail. Some ore never made it that far, given the number of damaged wagons that littered the tracks along the way. We saw our first vegetation in five hours at Managum when we entered an avenue of oleander bushes and eucalyptus trees so reminiscent of Australia. The entire landscape had a distinctive 'outback' feel to it, especially those parts of the land down under that are sandy desert. It increased the sense of connection I'd already begun to feel with this vast, seemingly empty terrain.

Shortly after Managum we drove through a gap in the escarpment and descended into an oasis. For the first time I began to understand what an oasis is. Far from the popularized Hollywood image of a cluster of date palms around a spring and a pond, oases are immense depressions in the desert plateau formed as a result of the combined action of wind, tectonics and water. They are near or at sea level where the massive reserves of underground water flowing north from central Africa come to the surface. The 2,000-square kilometer Bahariya depression is the smallest of the four major oases in the Western Desert. It is surrounded by several tiers of high escarpment which enclose a valley full of hills and mountains, some conical, some mesas, and others folded like the layers of an ancient garment.

One of the most dramatic parts of the Bahariya oasis is the White Desert near Farafara. Entering this area was like walking into a Salvador Dali painting. The numerous bleached, wind-eroded limestone sculptures gave the appearance of a bizarre collection of pieces on a gigantic chessboard. Arriving late afternoon, we were fortunate to experience the White Desert at three of its most enchanting moments — sunset, moonlight, and sunrise. Wandering among this surreal setting, I found a flat-topped piece about waist high and long enough to accommodate my body. I stripped to my underwear, hoisted myself atop the rock, and after checking for scorpions and other creatures, lay down on my towel. As the sun dipped below the horizon, the evening star appeared in a seamless transition. I wanted to capture and hold on to this precious moment but that was not to be. The air temperature quickly dropped, reminding me it was time to get dressed and rejoin the group.

While the days were a test of endurance with long drives in intense heat, the evenings were like a reward for our labors. Our first night in the desert we camped at Bir Ghaba, the Well in the Forest — 'forest' being a highly relative term. Situated on the old caravan route to Cairo, this popular well was shrouded in a grove of eucalyptus trees adjacent to a campsite operated by Bawiti's ironically named Alpenblick (view of the Alps) Hotel. Later that evening when the buzz around the campfire had died down to hushed whispers, I grabbed my towel and swimsuit and headed to the well. It was empty and silent, except for the torrent of water gushing out of the massive pipe at the deep end of the surrounding pool. As I lowered myself into the 38°C water, the moon appeared over the horizon in the most star-studded sky I had ever seen. The desert breeze, an ever-present companion, wafted through the trees. As I floated in the highly mineralized water I unloaded the six-day conference I had just come from, the never-ending book I was editing, and the long drive from Cairo.

We had two other opportunities during our trip to explore desert springs and wells. Although there are hundreds scattered throughout the oases, most are known only to locals and used by them for bathing and washing. Although some springs have cool water, many are hot, often severely so. One spring in Dakhla Oasis is said to be able to boil eggs. We tried our own egg boiler in Bahariya Oasis on our last night in the desert. With water at 45°C, Bir Ramla is the hottest spring in the oasis. While most of our group decided to pass, a few daring souls put their toes in the water to test the temperature. Shrieks filled the air. It reminded me of the copper cauldron in which we cooked crabs in when I was a boy. I took a deep breath and sank into the steaming water. While I've always handled hot water better than cold, this pushed me to my limits. After the initial shock my body adjusted to the intense heat, but I soon joined the others on the sidelines. I didn't want to become like the proverbial frog that boils itself to death while gradually adapting to the rising temperature.

Another spring captured my imagination in a totally different way. Known as the Magic Spring, it was identifiable by a lone clump of palm trees in an otherwise barren landscape. Our arrival at the Magic Spring came after a particularly harrowing ordeal. When we arrived at Bahariya, we transferred from our two minibuses into three Toyota jeeps to go on off-road excursions. A fourth jeep was our supply vehicle. On our second afternoon we were behind schedule and keen to arrive at our destination before sunset, so two of the drivers entered into a friendly race. The lead driver tried taking a short cut and strayed off course. As he started to descend a steep dune he lost control of the vehicle. It plummeted down the slope and rolled over before landing on its side. The other jeep arrived at the top of the dune seconds after, and seeing what had happened its driver managed to bring it to an abrupt halt.

A front-seat passenger, our oldest member, suffered cuts and abrasions to his head but others escaped injury. Built to withstand this kind of treatment, the jeeps came through in better shape. I was in the third vehicle, considerably behind the other two. We knew nothing about the accident, but when the faint sound of a horn kept repeating in the distance our driver sensed something was amiss. He entered into an intense discussion in Arabic with his companion but didn't divulge anything to the rest of us. When we joined the others and learned what had happened, a dramatic change of mood came over the whole group. After a brief discussion, the Egyptian crew decided to put 19 of us into two vehicles, while the supply truck went ahead to set up camp and the other jeep was retrieved from the bottom of the dune. By now it was pitch dark but remarkably the drivers managed to find the Magic Spring with nothing but headlights, their memory and instinct to guide them.

There was none of the usual singing and dancing that night, although a hearty meal of roast chicken and rice, along with an extra ration of beer, helped raise our spirits. The mood was subdued as we nursed our wounds and reflected on what we'd been through. We had had a hard lesson in the dangers that lurk just beneath the surface of this beguiling place. As we huddled together under camel hair blankets beneath a blazing sky, the silence of the desert enveloped us. Conversation died away as the last embers of the campfire glowed in the dark. Fennec foxes, hedgehogs and other animals that frequent this place stayed away that night. The Magic Spring cast its spell over us and sleep became our welcome friend.

Most evenings weren't so restrained. Reminiscent of scenes from the film *The English Patient*, we would gather after dinner around the campfire, sip mint tea or down a mildly warm beer, and let the show begin — the kind of show in which we were both audience and actor. To loosen us up, our Egyptian friends would ply us with rousing renditions of local folk tunes. The real act began when Mohammed, alias Baghdadi, took centre stage. With black, loose-fitting, drawstring pants and buttocks made for hard seats on long trips in fast-moving vehicles over rough terrain, he demonstrated the art of male belly dancing. Pounding the sand with his bare feet, he could move his middle body in gyrations that would rival those of many a professional female dancer.

Once Mohammed led the way, Reda and others followed. First among the foreigners to shed his European reticence was Cristian Nacht, who in his other life was the president of one of Brazil's largest steel construction companies. Clad in a flowing gray galabiya, Cristian tossed propriety to the wind, and with his feet and hips in sync, shuffled around the campfire like an old pro. After he'd broken the ice there was barely room to move, as the more timid among us took to the sand and made it sing.

While some found a way to escape this public celebration-cum-humiliation, there was one occasion when this was not possible. It was our last night in the desert before returning to

Cairo. We had traveled all afternoon, run out of fuel, and arrived at Bawiti tired, dirty and starving. After freshening up at the Hotel Alpenblick — where the water was running this time — we headed to the home of our host, Mohammed Ahmed el-Bayumi. El Bayumi was the proprietor of one of Bawiti's most popular restaurants, El Ghash (the Little Donkey). El Bayumi's reputation extended far beyond Bawiti or Bahariya Oasis. We had been warned that before entering the hallowed halls of his mud-floor establishment, we should be able to count to ten in Arabic or expect a clip over the ears. Should we master that feat we would be prime candidates to marry his sons or daughters, most of whom were in his employ.

But we had not been warned about El Bayumi's habit of blowing a shrill whistle to command the attention of his customers, like a sergeant-major drilling new recruits. Was this some ancient Bedouin custom or El Bayumi's way of asserting his dominance over this corralled band of foreigners? We first encountered this practice after our long drive from Cairo when we had lunch at El Ghash. Seated on the floor, we were eating and chatting among ourselves when El Bayumi strode into the room, let forth with his whistle, and asked in brusque Arabic, "Do you like my food?" Under the circumstances there seemed only one possible reply. We all agreed it was terrific.

Although we were now primed to expect the unexpected, none of us quite anticipated what El Bayumi had in store for us on this last night. The feast on the rooftop terrace of his sprawling home was a much grander affair than our earlier restaurant meal, with endless plates of barley soup, vegetable stew, roasted chicken, rice and hummus, along with plentiful supplies of beer. Our Egyptian guides decided it was their last chance to put their captive foreigners through the hoops. One by one, Baghdadi chose each of us to join him on the dance floor and get our bodies moving in time with the Bedouin music booming out of a ghetto blaster. Now and again a donkey would join in the festivities by braying loudly.

Next day as we contemplated our return to Cairo and our different countries, each of us reflected on this five-day excursion into what the Greek historian Herodotus called the 'Islands of the Blest.' Indeed, we had been blessed in a number of ways — the rich variety of time-tested landforms, the ever-welcome presence of water in the most surprising places, the engulfing silence of the starry desert nights. Most of all, we had been blessed by the irrepressible spirit of our Egyptian hosts. One experience captured this for me more than all others.

On our second day in the desert, after a quiet lunch in the shady palms of Ain el Ris (Spring of the Source), our convoy headed up the escarpment that marks the southern boundary of Bahariya Oasis. Although dunes cover 40 per cent of the Western Desert, they are not dominant in this oasis. This was our first encounter with these deceptively picturesque but potentially destructive desert landforms.

Of the four vehicles, the one I was in was the Cinderella of the group. Since it lacked a radiator cap, we had to stop frequently to let it cool and refill with water, which it consumed in endless quantities. On this occasion, the other three vehicles had reached the top of the dune and were watching us flail away in the sand. I couldn't tell whether their intermittent cheers were urging us on or lording it over us. Mahmoud, our driver, would thrust the gears into four-wheel drive, stomp on the accelerator, and let it fly. In Sisyphean style, we would make it almost to the top of the dune, peter out, and roll back down, only to have to repeat it.

At our fourth attempt we made it. Without hesitating Reda grabbed his drum and Mohammed his flute and goaded this motley group of sunburned foreigners into action. "Dance?

Did you say dance?" It was Zorba the Greek, Egyptian-style. It was time to rehearse that great Islamic expression, *insha' allah* — if God wills it. Clearly, Allah was willing a little celebration.

Some say the people of the Western Desert have a greater sense of humor and a more light-hearted spirit than inhabitants of other parts of Egypt. Those we encountered during these five days certainly possessed that and more. Their willingness to embrace life's mysteries and intrusions, its highs and lows, its blessings and curses was something to admire and emulate. It has, no doubt, enabled them to survive in unbelievably severe conditions for tens of thousands of years. It is not surprising, perhaps, that several of the world's religions emerged from places like this. If only a little of their spirit rubbed off on us during our brief encounter with the Western Desert we were so much the richer for it.

UTTERMOST
PART OF THE EARTH

· · · · ·

This journey had several beginnings. The first was Bruce
Chatwin's book *In Patagonia* about his quest to find the
cave visited by his great uncle. The second was the masterful
biography of Chatwin by Nicholas Shakespeare who retraced
Chatwin's footsteps and found variations in his subject's
account of his experiences. And there was the death of our
19-year-old dog, Ganesh, after which I wanted to take a long
trip to help grieve. But it turned out to be the other kind of
long — nearly 15,000 kilometers to Tierra del Fuego at the
tip of South America.

I resolved to do this after reading yet another book, E. Lucas Bridge's *Uttermost Part of the Earth*, first published in 1947. One of six children of Englishman Thomas Bridges, Lucas documented how his family settled Tierra del Fuego in the early 1800s, initially as missionaries and later as owners of cattle and sheep estancias. Their efforts to understand the indigenous peoples of this remote island, learn and record their languages, mediate in their disputes, and attempt to protect them from disease and annihilation set them apart from most Europeans of their day.

My husband, Bruce, accompanied me on this trip. As we flew from Buenos Aires to Ushuaia, capital of the Argentine half of the island, we followed the Atlantic coast most of the way. We hadn't anticipated the sheer size of Tierra del Fuego; after crossing its northeast corner we were still 20 minutes from landing on its south coast. Jutting out into a bay, Ushuaia's airport is a fortress of massive timber beams and steel girders anchored into stone and concrete to withstand Antarctic gales. After a short taxi ride from the airport we arrived at La Casa de Alba, where we found ourselves seated around a table with two other travelers. Alba was an attractive young woman with auburn hair and a no-nonsense manner. Thrusting maps of Ushuaia in front of us, she let forth her opening volley.

"You can have my bad English or my good Spanish. You decide! Understand?"

Being two Americans, an Australian and a Scotsman we settled for her bad English, which was very good. During her 30-minute spiel, she advised us where not to eat — "too much expensive; save your money" — and suggested tours and day trips, while writing notes on our maps like a teacher scribbling on your homework.

Alba strongly recommended us to take advantage of the current fine weather, so we booked a sail boat ride that afternoon down the Beagle Channel, including a stop at an island used for environmental research. The outward journey was so calm that we motored to the island, but later in the afternoon the wind had come up so we skimmed across the water full-sail back to port. When we arrived at the island the crew jumped onto a rocky promontory and tethered the boat while the rest of us hauled ourselves up the bank with a rope. It was then I noticed the name of our boat. Fuegans have a healthy sense of humor combined with a say-it-like-it-is attitude. 'No Top Hill' and 'Thought Of' peninsula — where Thomas Bridges thought of locating his estancia — are cases in point. But a yacht called 'If' gave me second thoughts.

The bird and plant life on Island H — yes, it was shaped like one — was abundant. The bolax ground cover like a giant green sponge, the vibrant red fire bush, and yellow lichen caught our attention. But we were most captivated by what appeared to be an abandoned campground with scattered animal bones, mussel shells and ash from campfires. As our guide described this ancient Indian midden we were swept back in time when the Yahgan Indians inhabited this area. A highly mobile people, they lived along the Beagle Channel and islands south to Cape Horn, hunting otter, fish and seals with spears and harpoons. They covered their naked bodies with seal oil to protect themselves from the cold and made canoes from tree bark. I had read about these amazingly hardy people but to sit where they had sat and handle their tools was a much more visceral experience.

The next day we decided to hike in the nearby national park. The higher altitude trek with beaver dams and gnarly lenga trees was manageable. The eight-kilometer shoreline walk was more of a test. But the third and final trail through peat bogs late in the day proved my undoing. Bruce chose to photograph a lake instead, but I was determined to push on to the end of National Route 3 that began 3,000 kilometers away in Buenos Aires. I made it to the terminus but when I tried to climb to a nearby lookout my knees seized up. I staggered back down just in time to catch our bus back to Ushuaia.

Next morning my legs were still protesting strongly but I promised them a reprieve since we had booked an off-road safari. At 8:30 am a white Land Rover pulled up outside Alba's front gate and we piled in, along with two Dutchmen and three Brazilian women. The Dutchmen were subdued but the Brazilians more than made up for them. Switching between Portuguese, Spanish and English they punctuated every sentence with howls of laughter. It felt like a good team, along with Pablo, our driver-cum-guide.

We sped out of town past Mount Olivia that soars like a giant watch tower at Ushuaia's eastern gateway. After that the road climbed steadily for 45 minutes before we came to Garibaldi Pass, where we stood awestruck by the yawning vista before us. Below was Lago Escondido where we would return later in the day to kayak. In the far distance was the sprawling Lago Fagnano, our lunch destination accessible only by four-wheel-drive vehicles.

I've lived in remote places where 'track' is a loosely used term, but I was not prepared for what we encountered once we left the asphalt. The track quickly disintegrated into mud bogs that would challenge the most earnest rally driver. At one point Pablo stopped the vehicle and had everyone get out while he put the Land Rover to the test. As he did so, another vehicle joined us, so we proceeded in convoy for half an hour until we glimpsed the lakeshore. At the top of the final crest Pablo pressed down on the accelerator and drove at breakneck speed into the water. The Brazilian chorus shrieked with delight as our now-amphibious vehicle created waves.

Pablo steered the Land Rover along the lakeshore for several kilometers until we came to a dirt track that led into the forest. Back on land, the vehicles disgorged their passengers while the drivers prepared a classic Argentine barbecue. It was good to be on solid ground and settle our stomachs before submitting them to a grand repast of appetizers, wall-to-wall meat, salads, bread, dessert and plentiful red wine.

By the next day my legs had partially recovered but another test was in store. Behind Ushuaia lies the majestic Martial Glacier. A 15-minute taxi ride from town deposited us at the base of a chairlift. As we ascended, the valley below and the Beagle Channel beyond opened up like a giant IMAX screen. From the terminus of the chairlift it was another 45-minute walk to the base of the glacier, from where we looked back to the tree line below. Recalling Alba's warning about the changeability of the weather, we decided not to linger and headed down a forest trail back to town. During the two-hour trek we saw no-one but acquired a dog who insisted on accompanying us to the outskirts of Ushuaia.

The following day the weather worsened, so we decided to visit the Museo Maritimo and Museo del Presidio. Designed like the spokes of a wheel, the building was constructed between 1906 and 1920 as a prison for, and by, some of Argentina's hard-core convicts. Built to house 380 prisoners, it held up to 800 at its peak and was closed in 1947. I was drawn to the wing devoted to Antarctic exploration, in which Ushuaia has played an important role. Since it is the closest point to Antarctica, many countries used this as their base to explore the southernmost latitudes. Cruise ships have now replaced sailings ships to take visitors to the white continent during the southern summer.

* * *

The evening before departing on our road trip we went to the rental agency to collect our car. As we approached we noticed a young man hosing down a small vehicle that had been rear-ended and whose windshield had been gashed by a stone. We didn't pay much attention to it since we had ordered another make and model. Alas, this Volkswagen Gol was indeed our car, since there wasn't another. It seemed like a downgrade, not an upgrade. Next morning we hadn't left the town limits when we heard a loud scraping noise in low gear. Bruce and I exchanged nervous glances. Should we go back or proceed? After driving at faster speeds the sound receded, so we decided to risk it.

First stop was Estancia Harberton, home to the Bridges-Goodall family and the oldest house in Argentine Tierra del Fuego. The original homestead was prefabricated in England and assembled here. It had been modified over the years but still retained its simple, rustic charm with wooden beams and a corrugated iron façade. It housed much of the Bridges family legacy and is an Argentine National Historical Monument. We stayed in the old Cook House, whose iron beds and wooden furniture were family antiques and we ate meals in the Casa de Té, site of the original kitchen and now an office. Like all buildings in the estancia, it was full of photos, maps and memorabilia from its rich past.

But for Saturday night dinner we were invited to join the family in the old dining room. Hosted by Tom and Natalie Goodall, the senior generation of the Bridges-Goodall family at Harberton, we were swept back to pioneering days vividly described in *Uttermost Part of the Earth*. Seated at the original dining room table, we ate food from the kitchen that had prepared meals for more than 120 years. Indian arrowheads and fishbone spears adorned the walls, along with an old telephone in one corner and a bookcase of family treasures. As

Tom carved the roast at one end of the table, Natalie presided at the other. Conversation flowed in English and Spanish among three generations of family members, student interns and guests.

We plied Natalie with so many questions that after dinner she asked if Bruce and I would like to see a slide show of Harberton's history. We leaped at the opportunity to further acquaint ourselves with this extraordinary family. As Natalie commented on each photo, stories unfolded — the shipwrecked French sailors who appeared one night on their doorstep, the visit of Charles Darwin's great-grandson, Bruce Chatwin's brief stopover, early flying adventures, and more. It was an evening we didn't want to end.

After breakfast next morning I asked Natalie what else I might read about Harberton and the people who forged it. She invited us into the library and produced book after book, before presenting us with a signed copy of her own bilingual volume on Tierra del Fuego. We could have spent weeks here but had arranged to stay at the other family estancia that night and had a ferry reservation across the Magellan Strait the day after. As Natalie was showing us a copy of *The Falklands Islands Journal* — an encyclopedic collection of articles on the history of the region — Tom asked if we would like to see more. After a nod from us he disappeared into a nearby room and returned with a CD containing 40 years of the journal.

As well as having married into the Bridges-Goodall family, Natalie was a highly respected marine biologist who collaborated with scientists in other southern hemisphere countries. The museum of birds and sea mammals she established on the property housed more than 4,000 species, including a variety of whale skeletons. Specimens were stored in a nearby bone house until they were cleaned, processed and taken to the laboratory. Constanza, one of a number of graduate students whom Natalie supervised, captivated us with an hour-long, personalized tour of the museum and laboratory. This celebrated historic outpost was continuing to probe new frontiers.

Our next stop was Viamonte ('through the woods'), the second Bridges estancia about 200 kilometers north on the Atlantic coast. Compared to Harberton, snugly located on a peninsula in the Beagle Channel, Viamonte was within spitting distance of the ocean and exposed to the elements. It was established in 1902 by the sons of Thomas Bridges at the request of the Ona (Selknam) people to protect them from European incursions. As we sped along National Route 3, I was reminded of Lucas's account of how this trail was forged. He, his brothers and a number of Indians had hacked their way through lenga forest, forded rivers, and traversed peat bogs to carve out the route. Several years later Thomas Bridge's wife Mary, the clan matriarch, wanted to see Viamonte before returning to England to die. Her initial voyage from England had been such an ordeal that she refused ever to sail again. Ona men made a sedan chair and carried her the whole way.

Upon arrival at Viamonte we were greeted warmly by Carolina Goodall and her two charming daughters. It felt like meeting long-lost cousins, a feeling that persisted throughout our stay. Carolina and her husband Simon operated the estancia with other family members and employees. On its 40,500 hectares they ran 20,000 sheep and had the largest shearing shed I've ever seen. Since we had limited time, we decided to take a walk around the property straight away, aided by Carolina's hand-drawn map. Our destination was 'the house on wheels'.

"It's just a couple of kilometers. You can't miss it," said Carolina. "Take the main track as far as the big gate, then follow the fence line and just when you think you have gone too far, there it will be."

As we set out clouds were rolling in off the ocean but they didn't look too threatening. Before we left the homestead we noticed a small wooden hut that looked strangely familiar. It was no more than two by four meters with doors on both sides and small window openings. My mind flashed back to a photo in *Uttermost Part of the Earth* of the original hut built by Lucas and his Ona friends. This tiny structure housed four women and three children — the men slept outside — until the main homestead was built. By contrast, our spacious guestroom with its attached bathroom and giant claw-foot bathtub seemed ridiculously large.

As we walked we saw our first guanacos, close relatives of llamas, and a number of birds. But after more than an hour we hadn't come across a 'house on wheels'. Just as we were ready to call it quits, we turned a corner and there it stood — a cross between a railway coach and a gypsy carriage, sitting high off the ground and with a chimney poking out the roof. Inside were wooden bunks, a stove, kitchen, bathing area and cupboards. With stunning views of a sweeping valley it was tempting to linger here, but the clouds had intensified and we had a long walk back to the homestead.

The track petered out shortly after so we contemplated turning back. Just at that moment, I thought I heard voices. We stopped, listened and walked a little further. Then we spotted a group of people and a pick-up truck parked in the trees. We could barely believe our luck. Scouring my mind for my best phrasebook Spanish I approached one of the group.

"*Hola*," I said. "*Me he perdido*." (Hello. I am lost.)

In what sounded remarkably like an American accent the other person replied, "No, you're not lost. Let me show you the way."

The voice's owner turned out to be Tomas, a Viamonte staff member who had married into the family. He was picnicking with friends and assured us we only had to follow the tree line and we would make it back to the homestead. We thanked Tomas and moved on, not quite believing our good fortune.

The clouds now looked ominous and rain started falling, so we stepped up our pace, keeping close to the tree line for shelter. Then the track veered into open land, across several fences and over countless hillocks. Each time we reached a summit we were sure we would see the homestead, but that wasn't to be. The rain grew heavier. Herds of cattle appeared and stampeded in all directions. In the far distance we could faintly make out the road with matchbox-size vehicles on it. If all else failed we would make for that.

Soaked to the skin, we pushed on. As we came to the top of the next rise a truck appeared about a hundred meters ahead. We ran towards it, thinking it may not have seen us. We needn't have worried. It was Tomas and one of his guests. They abandoned their picnic because of the rain, but when they discovered we hadn't returned they came to find us. As we drove back to the homestead Tomas told us he had worked as manager of Ted Turner's ranch in Montana. He regaled us with stories of the millionaire media magnate — and largest individual landowner in the Americas — and his actress wife, Jane Fonda. Before depositing us at our guesthouse he gave us a tour of the homestead and surrounds. We anointed him Saint Tomas.

Next morning over breakfast our waitress informed us that a special visitor was about to join us. Within minutes an older man with a reddish face and loose strands of white hair ambled into the room. He introduced himself as Adrian Goodall, brother of Tom whom we had met at Harberton. Adrian and his wife were the senior residents at Viamonte. He was friendly, humorous, unpretentious and eager to help any way he could. As we ate he fed us more stories about this enthralling part of the world and the role the Bridges/Goodall family had played in it.

After breakfast we went over our planned route across the island. We were headed for Porvenir, a town of 5,000 on the Magellan Strait that is the capital of Chilean Tierra del Fuego. Between Viamonte and Porvenir were 280 kilometers of mostly unpaved road, a border crossing, and no refueling stops after the town of Rio Grande. We needed local advice and Adrian rose to the occasion. Since we had to spend a night in Porvenir we asked if he could recommend a place to stay. After making a couple of phone calls he returned with several suggestions and a recommendation.

Going from Argentina to Chile was one of the more relaxed border crossings I've experienced. No forbidding glass screens, no soldiers or security police, no dogs sniffing under your vehicle. We drove up to the Argentine customs and immigration building at San Sebastián (Argentina), parked our car, and sauntered over to the desk. The procedure was simple and efficient, since we were returning to Argentina in a few days. In addition to having our rental car papers stamped and signed, we had to fill out a small form in quadruplicate. The immigration officer took the first copy and handed us the other three. We went back to our car, drove through the unattended barrier, and crossed 11 kilometers to the Chilean border post at San Sebastián (Chile). Here we re-presented the triplicate form, from which they extracted the second copy. On our return several days later the same procedure was done in reverse.

The paperwork was a breeze but the road between the two control posts was a nightmare. This no man's land was unpaved and after the luxury of National Route 3 it was a shock to the system — ours and our Volkswagen Gol. It was a bone-rattler of the highest order, reminiscent of roads in outback Australia.

Throughout the day we passed few vehicles and encountered one broken down. We wondered what we'd do if ours did. There was no cell phone reception and homesteads were far apart. Only late in the day, as the road angled down to the shimmering waters of the Magellan Strait, did it improve. It felt like a reward for endurance.

Porvenir ('the future') was just that for the early Croatian settlers who flocked to the town when gold was found in 1879. The gold dwindled but the Croatians stayed, to become the backbone of thriving fishing and sheep industries. We soon found Adrian's recommended Hotel Rosas, where we were warmly greeted by its owner, Alberto, who nodded approvingly at the mention of Señor Goodall of Viamonte. I came to appreciate this pleasant little man who listened patiently as Bruce and I struggled with our Spanish. When we dined that night in the hotel restaurant Alberto was our chef and waiter, other roles he played with great aplomb.

One could easily mistake Porvenir for an insignificant town of corrugated iron houses and government offices but it impressed us for one reason in particular — the number of sculptures and memorials in honor of the region's original inhabitants, the Ona (Selknam) people. Known for their large stature, the Ona hunted with bows and arrows and were skilled woodsmen. They wore robes and moccasins made from guanaco skins and carried children in cradles. It was probably their fires that Magellan saw in 1520 when he first came through the strait that bears his name and led him to name the island Tierra de los Fuegos, Land of Fires. Many Ona were killed in clashes with Europeans or infighting, but even more died of introduced diseases. Only mixed-raced descendants survive today.

Our trip across the Magellan Strait filled me with anticipation and trepidation. When I booked our passage I was warned that the boat may not sail due to bad weather. But the next day greeted us with clear skies and a light breeze. As we drove to the dock I was surprised to see the blue car ferry with the name *Cruz Australis* (Southern Cross). I was not expecting such a large, modern vessel and not one with such a familiar name. We drove our little Gol into the ship's gaping jaws, along with SUVs, buses and semi-trailers. Once parked, we headed to the passenger lounge with its spacious seats, snack bar, and television monitors with the latest Chilean soap operas. But our attention was quickly diverted to a pod of dolphins that escorted us out of the harbor into the strait, as if to farewell us from the island.

Our arrival in Punta Arenas on mainland Chile was a shock. After ten days of small towns and rustic estancias, we found ourselves in a city of 130,000 people with multi-lane roads, stern-looking colonial buildings and elegant parks. As we drove to our bed-and-breakfast, Bruce and I had the same reaction — this is not where we want to spend our time! Our main reason for staying was to meet British travel writer and animal lover, Lorraine Chittock, who had driven with her two dogs from the US through Central and South America on one of her epic safaris, later to be documented in the beautiful book *Los Mutts*. I was looking forward to meeting Lorraine after communicating with her for many years but she and her canine companions had headed north just two days before.

Early next morning we drove to the penguin colony at Seno Otway (Otway Sound). After missing the turn-off from the main road, enduring 45 minutes of rough gravel and paying a landowner to drive through his property, we were confronted by a most unusual sight — two parallel roads on either side of a fence. One took us to the penguin colony while the other belonged to a mining company. By the time we arrived at the colony some of the adult penguins had already gone to sea on their daily feeding mission, leaving their partners standing guard at their nests. It was a touching sight. But when we reached the shoreline we were confronted by hundreds of penguins jabbering away like a herd of braying donkeys.

We had planned to spend another two nights in Chile but it was not to be. Our map indicated many places marked 'hotel' or 'hostel' but they never materialized. Fortunately, that day we had treated ourselves to a hearty lunch, something we don't usually do. We were lured by *Lonely Planet*'s glowing review of Estancia Rio Verde on the shores of Seno Skyring (Skyring Sound). Their lunch of Patagonian lamb, freshly baked bread, garden vegetables and wine for CH$5,000 (US$8.50) seemed too good to be true. We didn't bother to check the price when we ordered, so when the bill came to far more than that we were shocked. Credit cards were not an option. Luckily we had just enough pesos to cover the bill and save us embarrassment.

Stomachs fortified and heads a little light, we drove on to the small town of Villa Tehuelches. Given time and distances we decided this was as far north as we should go. After an abortive effort to locate an archaeological site our spirits began to flag, when Bruce signaled frantically to our right. In the middle of a lake was a huge flock of pink flamingos. We'd read about flamingos in this part of the country but never thought we'd see any. We continued along the northern shore of the Magellan Strait, known for its unpredictable weather that made it treacherous for shipping. This was brought home to us in dramatic fashion at the abandoned town of San Gregorio, where we stopped to examine the wrecks of a tea clipper and a steamer.

Assuming we would find somewhere to stay the night we kept driving, but after checking two more locations without success we grew concerned. Our only option was to head back to Tierra del Fuego via the narrow crossing at Punta Delgada. Once back on the island we headed for the only town in the entire northeast, Cerro Sombrero (Hat Hill), operated by the Chilean national petroleum company. According to *Lonely Planet* there was accommodation in this town, but what this meant didn't sink in until we arrived at the Hosteria Tunkelen. Not only was this the only place to stay in town, its restaurant was the only place to eat. Moreover, the restaurant had a set menu, mostly for company employees. Next morning when we went to fill up our car for the long drive south, the only gas available was at a single pump operated, of course, by the company.

As we strolled around town after dinner we thought we had stepped back into a 1960s Soviet-style community where everything was provided for the workers, from an Olympic-size swimming pool and gymnasium to a cinema and gigantic outdoor chessboard. The chessboard was next to the supermarket, which was next to the bank and post office, which was next to the workers' club and over the road from the high school. Company housing varied from bungalows to dormitories. The whole town seemed surreal in a benign kind of way. We were glad to have found a place to spend the night but equally glad to leave, not knowing we were taking a memento with us. For the following two days we both had severe diarrhea.

We headed back to Ushuaia to recover before our flight home. We were warned to avoid the heavily traveled truck route from Cerro Sombrero to San Sebastián, so chose a secondary road instead. We were glad we did, since the route took us through rolling hills where we saw guanacos, a rhea and a Fuegan fox, as well as lots of cattle. At one point we came to a T-junction, in the middle of which stood a shed big enough for one person. What was it for, we wondered?

Was it a bus stop, a pickup point or something else? It seemed emblematic of the serendipity we had come to associate with this incredible island. As we came over Garibaldi Pass and descended to Ushuaia it felt like coming home, although we'd only landed there 11 days before. Our beloved Gol had survived 1,500 kilometers without mishap.

Our last day in Ushuaia was a chance to reflect on our journey. When I read E. Lucas Bridge's book I had an inexplicable sense of connection with this distant part of the world, which was reinforced by my visit there. Part of that was due to its many parallels with Australia — its role as a prison colony, its shameful treatment of its indigenous peoples, its huge sheep estancias and more. But it went deeper. Tierra del Fuego is a place that pushes human endurance to its limits, whose savage beauty and fickle climate make one respectful of nature, and which attracts those who dare to break out of their comfort zones and cross the boundaries life has prescribed for them. There is no greater exemplar of this than the Bridges family whose life embodied their name and whose legacy proudly remains in this uttermost part of the earth.

Afterword

. . . . .

Having visited more than 40 countries, I've never failed to be impressed by how many Australians and New Zealanders I've encountered. Except for Germans, who travel widely thanks to their generous holidays and whose population is more than three times Australia's, antipodean adventurers punch way above their weight. From Lima to Lombok, Tokyo to Timbuktu they keep showing up. So I was surprised to read recently that only 57 percent of Australians own a passport and only 40 percent have been abroad. What happened to that craving for adventure that made the overland trek to Europe or an extended 'working holiday' such a rite of passage to adulthood in the 1960s and 70s?

Yet I was pleased to discover that increasingly young Australians are taking a 'gap year' between school and further studies. According to one researcher, the gap year is not just a time to blow off steam or escape home pressures, but a chance to crystallize decisions about one's future, develop personal skills, and increase self-confidence. How I could have used such a thing at that age. While some will tell you they knew what they wanted to do with their lives when they were five or six, not I. I was rudderless and indecisive at 17, let alone at 21 after completing four years of university. I had vague notions of becoming a diplomat, urban planner, sociolinguist, journalist and clergyman but none was compelling enough to capture me. Neither did academia. When two professors each suggested I do post-graduate studies, I politely declined. I was yearning for something else, but what?

My 'gap year' turned out to be my trip to America in 1971, which transformed the term 'culture shock' from something abstract to utterly real. It was culture shock on three levels simultaneously — American culture, ghetto society and the Institute itself. A baptism of fire doesn't come close to describing it. Had I been more self-driven and less other-directed I might have chalked up my year in America as a useful learning experience and returned to Australia. Instead, my gap year turned out to be the beginning of a much longer journey that continues to this day.

Travel has been an important part of that journey and still is. It opens doors, challenges stereotypes, builds bridges and expands the mind. As travel writer and guide Rick Steves put it, "it moves around your furniture." It also taps into something more fundamental in our lives, as author Bruce Chatwin — who rejected the label of being a 'travel writer' — said. "The act of journeying contributes towards a sense of physical and mental well-being, while the monotony of prolonged settlement or regular work weaves patterns in the brain that engender fatigue and a sense of personal inadequacy." While Chatwin's renowned global meanderings dwarf mine, his words ring true. Travel has energized me and given me a sense of connection that makes me thirst for more.

Roland Joffé, director of Academy Award-winning movies *The Killing Fields* and *The Mission,* points to another aspect of travel that is often overlooked. "When we leave our homelands, we unmoor, we unstick from all those routines that kind of keep us ourselves. And a lot of acting out begins to happen...Everyone who goes and lives abroad...begins to discover aspects of themselves, different ways of behaving that probably they weren't aware of when they were at home in their own countries." Never was this truer for me than the years I spent in India, when I found myself on a journey of sexual self-discovery that changed the course of my life.

My journeying began at a tender age. As a child I was drawn to atlases and stamps that allowed my imagination to transport me to places beyond my known world. Few ten-year-olds could tell you that the Pennine Chain was in the UK while the Apennines were in Italy, but I could. I poured over maps and memorized geographical trivia as if my life depended on it. No place took precedence over others; all were fair game for my sponge of a mind. Little did I know that these flights of fancy were preparing me to visit many of these places and meet their inhabitants, as well as live and work in several.

Traveling has taught me a number of things and continues to do so. First, travel is about people, not places. It is the connections you make and the relationships you form that make travel worthwhile, and sometimes, possible. Few stories illustrate this better than my 1995 trip to Jamaica to watch a cricket match between Australia and the West Indies. Ten days before I left home I hadn't conceived of this trip. Little did I imagine then that I would sit in the press box, be invited to the official reception, or be accommodated in a luxury apartment. This all happened because of a string of people including generous former colleagues, an earnest magazine editor, and a trusting secretary of the West Indian Cricket Association.

Second, should you show up in a place unexpectedly, do not assume you are unwelcome. Indeed, the opposite may be the case. In cultures that place a high value on hospitality your presence is often seen as a blessing. India has a wonderful expression for this: The guest is a god. So often in India I would be given the best bed and fed the finest food, no matter how poor my hosts. Invariably people would want me to stay longer and I'd have to excuse myself. Those who live more circumscribed lives often welcome, even yearn for, an injection of otherness into their daily routines. Having lived in a small island community for the last 20 years, I've come to appreciate this. As much as we enjoy old friends and neighbors, dinner party conversations with them tend to follow fairly predictable patterns. Interacting with newcomers not only expands our horizons, but can reveal surprising connections and allow us to rehearse and reaffirm our own lives.

Third, hospitality may be freely given but often comes with unspoken expectations. I was reminded of this when I stayed with a British missionary couple in Livingstone, Zambia, near Victoria Falls. I'd been given their name by a co-worker who told me they were not well off but would be good for a bed and perhaps a little breakfast. As soon as I made their acquaintance I felt uneasy because it was apparent they lived a very frugal life. So on my first night, which happened to be my birthday, I ate out in town. The next day my hostess berated me for not having dinner with them the night before — even though she had not invited me. My bumbling apology about not wanting to impose on their goodwill didn't go over very well, so I made amends the following evening. When we discovered we had a common acquaintance from our past my faux pas was forgiven and equanimity was restored.

Fourth, a guest can play many roles — the bringer of news, the teller of stories, the curious outsider, the interested listener and more. But whatever your role, finding ways to build bridges between you and your host is key. This can be as simple as asking a question or acknowledging what the other person has said, or it may require more. Finding points of commonality and using those to enhance your connection with your host can be a great help. In India the thing I most often used to do this was cricket. My own love of the game didn't come close to that or your average Indian. Countless times on buses or trains, waiting in a queue or sitting on a park bench, the mere mention of the word 'cricket' would create an instant bond between me and the other person. On one occasion it led to a chef in a five-star hotel inviting my mother and me to dine at his fine establishment. Another time, on a fundraising call, a donor not only upped his annual contribution but invited me to be his guest at his exclusive club.

Fifth, knowing even a smattering of the local language is a great asset, practically and symbolically. Polite words and phrases never go astray and basic commands and requests are always useful. But there is one sentence I have found to be key to master — Your food is delicious. Invariably it brought smiles from my hosts, particularly women who, in many cultures, not only cook and serve food but often are subjugated to the background. Food is so inextricably linked to culture that appreciating it is honoring the culture. Sometimes, however, praising your host's cuisine requires detachment from one's own cultural predilections. On a visit to a village in Côte d'Ivoire a colleague and I were guests of the chief who ordered a grand repast to be prepared in our honor. While I've eaten almost-raw crocodile and charred kangaroo, I'd never tasted agouti or cane rat, an Ivorian delicacy. Seeing agouti body parts floating in the fiery stew and dissecting meat from its three-toed feet pushed me to the edge of my comfort zone.

Finally, traveling to different parts of the world I've found it helpful to visit neighboring countries in order to see one from the perspective of the other. Even if they shared the same colonial masters and have similar cultural roots, countries often evolved differently. I found this to be true of India and Bangladesh, Zambia and Zimbabwe, Nigeria and Côte d'Ivoire. Although I lived and worked in India for six years, it wasn't until I visited Bangladesh in 1984 that I fully realized how much of an economic giant India is. While India produced everything from matchsticks to spacecraft, Bangladesh still imported many basic commodities. I was frequently told that the country's most productive industry was foreign aid. Given the size of Bangladesh's extensive NGO community this may well have been correct. Two years later when I was in Zambia, empty supermarket shelves depicted a country in dire economic straits, while neighboring Zimbabwe was regarded as one of Africa's few economic success stories. Zambia's lot has since improved but Zimbabwe's sadly has slipped dramatically.

* * *

From my youngest days travel has been an intrinsic part of my life that I've come to see as a 'quest for the other.' It took me years to connect the dots but once I did a pattern began to emerge. It was probably not by chance that my best friend in primary school was a boy of Indo-Burmese descent, my best mate at university was Chinese Malaysian, and that I once dated a young Aboriginal woman. It was probably not happenstance that for my undergraduate major I chose anthropology — the study of human society and culture in its myriad forms. And it was probably not surprising that when I finally came to terms with my homosexuality, I was living and working in India.

Growing up in 1950s–70s Australia as a white, Anglo-Saxon male I was part of the majority culture. Multiculturalism was years away from becoming the dominant theme in Australian life it is today. While my gestures to seek out 'the other' in the mainstream culture were just that — gestures — they were preparing me for a lifelong journey in which I would find myself being 'the other' in a variety of settings. And not just exotic places like a Chicago black ghetto, a remote Australian

Aboriginal community or Indian villages, but as a gay husband and stepfather in suburban Seattle and as a foreign resident on a small island in the Pacific Northwest.

While travel has exposed me to the world's diversity and given me opportunities others could only yearn for, it has also raised questions of identity and belonging, particularly as I've grown older. Although I still find it hard to resist the lure of the unknown and long to cross more frontiers, one day my travels will end. What will I have gained from my peripatetic life? What will it have taught me about myself, as well as the world? And what legacy do I wish to leave? I admire those who, like Australian writer Tim Winton, have a deep attachment to a particular place or part of the world. As he wrote in his highly evocative memoir, *Land's Edge*, "There is nowhere else I'd rather be, nothing else I would prefer to be doing. I am at the beach looking west with the continent behind me as the sun tracks down to the sea. I have my bearings." The closest I come to Winton's steadfastness is feeling a tug on my heartstrings and tears in my eyes when I hear Peter Allen's classic song *I Still Call Australia Home*, no doubt because I don't still call it home.

As much as I might long for such a deep attachment to one corner of this planet, it eludes me. When I recently had to give instructions for the disposal of my remains I found myself conflicted. How could I choose just one place, when home has been so many places for me? I finally settled on dividing up my remains between three places that have been pivotal in my life. I am a person of many parts and have found inspiration from many quarters, and as much as I revel in the particular I feel the pull of the universal. I always have and probably always will.

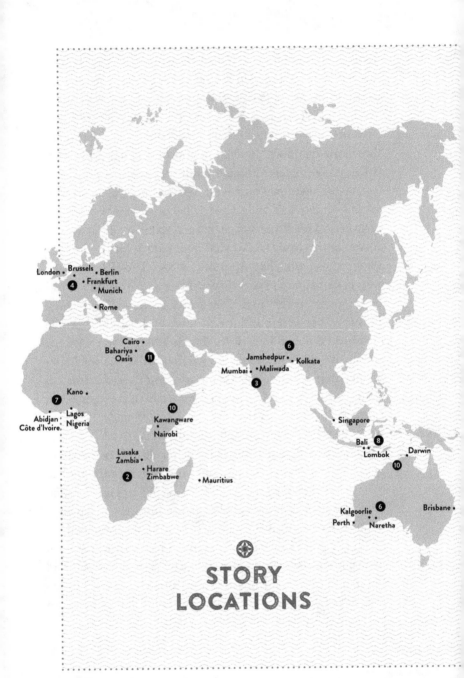

STORY
LOCATIONS

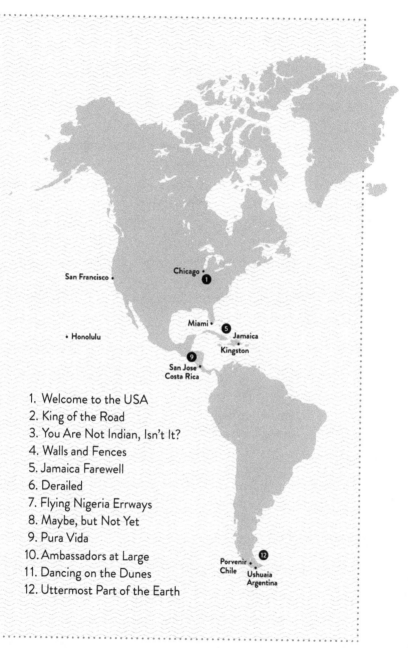

San Francisco •

Chicago •
1

Miami •
5
Jamaica

• Honolulu

Kingston

San Jose •
Costa Rica
9

Porvenir •
Chile
12
Ushuaia
Argentina

Photographic Credits

Notes

1. All measurements are metric. The following conversions
   may assist readers not familiar with the metric system:
   1 centimeter = 0.39 inches
   1 hectare = 2.47 acres
   1 meter = 1.09 yards
   1 kilometer = 0.62 mile
   1 square kilometer = 0.39 square miles
   0° Celsius = 32° Fahrenheit (x 9/5 + 32)

2. Spelling is American English usage.

3. The names Bombay and Calcutta have been used to reflect
   the era in which the story was set.

About the Author

Australian-born John Burbidge has visited more than 40 countries and lived in five. His homes have included a Chicago ghetto, an Australian Aboriginal community and Indian villages. Graduating from university in 1971, he joined an international NGO  that pioneered people's participation in community and organizational development. After playing many roles from facilitator to fundraiser to communications director, he left after 30 years to pursue his own writing. He is the author of an acclaimed biography of Australian writer Gerald Glaskin and a memoir of coming out as a gay man in India. He lives with his husband in Washington state, USA.

Websites:
www.wordswallah.com
www.geraldglaskin.com
www.theboatmanamemoir.com

9 780578 698144